First World War
and Army of Occupation
War Diary
France, Belgium and Germany

47 DIVISION
142 Infantry Brigade
London Regiment
22nd (County of London) Battalion (The Queen's)
1 September 1918 - 2 May 1919

WO95/2732/5

The Naval & Military Press Ltd
www.nmarchive.com
Published in association with The National Archives

Published by

The Naval & Military Press Ltd

Unit 10 Ridgewood Industrial Park,

Uckfield, East Sussex,

TN22 5QE England

Tel: +44 (0) 1825 749494

www.naval-military-press.com

www.nmarchive.com

This diary has been reprinted in facsimile from the original. Any imperfections are inevitably reproduced and the quality may fall short of modern type and cartographic standards.

© Crown Copyright
Images reproduced by permission of The National Archives, London, England, 2015.

Contents

Document type	Place/Title	Date From	Date To
Heading	WO95/2732 Sept'18-May'19 1/22 London R		
Heading	47th Division 142nd Infy Bde 1-22nd London Regt Sept 1918-May 1919		
Heading	1/22 London Rgt Vol 28 June 1917		
Heading	On His Majesty's Service. Duplicate War Diary 3/1/16 to 30/4/16 D.A.G. Base		
War Diary	Aderlu Wood	01/09/1918	01/09/1918
War Diary	Bouchavesnes	02/09/1918	02/09/1918
War Diary	West of Moislains	03/09/1918	03/09/1918
War Diary	Canal Bank	04/09/1918	06/09/1918
War Diary	Bouchavesnes	07/09/1918	07/09/1918
War Diary	Clery Sur Somme	08/09/1918	08/09/1918
War Diary	Mericourt L'Abbe	09/09/1918	09/09/1918
War Diary	Ecquedeques	10/09/1918	12/09/1918
War Diary	Lozinghem	13/09/1918	19/09/1918
War Diary	Conteville And Berthonval	20/09/1918	21/09/1918
War Diary	Conteville	22/09/1918	29/09/1918
War Diary	Framecourt Pt Houvin Ecoivres.	28/09/1918	30/09/1918
Heading	War Diary 1/22nd Bn The London Regt (The Queens) October 1918 Vol 44		
War Diary	Framecourt Ecoivres & Pt. Houvin	01/10/1918	02/10/1918
War Diary	Lagorgue	03/10/1918	03/10/1918
War Diary	Faucissart	03/10/1918	03/10/1918
War Diary	Fromelle	04/10/1918	04/10/1918
War Diary	In Line	04/10/1918	05/10/1918
War Diary	Le Maisnil	06/10/1918	08/10/1918
War Diary	Front Line	09/10/1918	11/10/1918
War Diary	Le Maisnil	12/10/1918	15/10/1918
War Diary	In Line	16/10/1918	17/10/1918
War Diary	Fosse	18/10/1918	18/10/1918
War Diary	Bourecq	19/10/1918	26/10/1918
War Diary	Loos	26/10/1918	28/10/1918
War Diary	Hellemmes	29/10/1918	31/10/1918
Operation(al) Order(s)	1/22nd Bn The London Regt Order No 203.	02/10/1918	02/10/1918
Miscellaneous	Appendix No 2. Order 204.		
Operation(al) Order(s)	1/22nd Bn The London Regt Order No 204.	03/10/1918	03/10/1918
Heading	War Diary 1/22nd Bn The London Regt November 1918.		
War Diary	Hellemmes	01/11/1918	01/11/1918
War Diary	Rue Franche	02/11/1918	07/11/1918
War Diary	Front Line	08/11/1918	09/11/1918
War Diary	Advancing		
War Diary	Advancing	10/11/1918	10/11/1918
War Diary	Moustiers	11/11/1918	11/11/1918
War Diary	Bizencourt & Bourgage	12/11/1918	13/11/1918
War Diary	Latombe	14/11/1918	15/11/1918
War Diary	Cysoing	16/11/1918	25/11/1918
War Diary	Havbourdin	26/11/1918	26/11/1918
War Diary	Bethune	27/11/1918	27/11/1918
War Diary	Ecquedecques	28/11/1918	30/11/1918

Heading	War Diary 1/22nd Bn London Regt December 1918		
War Diary	Ecquedecques	01/12/1918	31/12/1918
War Diary	Ecquedecques near Lillers	01/01/1919	16/01/1919
War Diary	Ecquedecques near Lillers	14/01/1919	16/01/1919
War Diary	Le Reveillon Camp near Allonampe	17/01/1919	17/01/1919
War Diary	Le Reveillon Camp	17/01/1919	30/01/1919
War Diary	Le Reveillon Camp Near Lillers	30/01/1919	31/01/1919
War Diary	Le Reveillion Camp	01/02/1919	03/02/1919
War Diary	Le Reveillion Allouagne	04/02/1919	09/02/1919
War Diary	Le Reveillion	10/02/1919	13/02/1919
War Diary	Le Reveillion Allouagne	14/02/1919	18/02/1919
War Diary	Le Reveillion	19/02/1919	22/02/1919
War Diary	Le Reveillion Allouagne	23/02/1919	28/02/1919
War Diary	Le Reveillion Allouagne	17/02/1919	17/02/1919
War Diary	Le Reveillon	01/03/1919	17/04/1919
War Diary	Fzoringhem	18/04/1919	29/04/1919
War Diary	Harfleur	30/04/1919	02/05/1919
Miscellaneous	A Form. Messages And Signals.		
Miscellaneous	2nd Batt. London Regt. H.Q. 140 Infantry Bde.	04/12/1918	04/12/1918
Miscellaneous	Appendix No 3. Order No 205.		
Operation(al) Order(s)	1/22nd Bn. London Regt Order No 205	03/10/1918	03/10/1918
Miscellaneous	Appendix No 4. Order No 206		
Operation(al) Order(s)	1/22nd Bn The London Regt Order No 206		
Miscellaneous	Appendix No 5 Order No 207		
Operation(al) Order(s)	1/22nd Bn London Regt Order No 207.	05/10/1918	05/10/1918
Miscellaneous	Schedule		
Miscellaneous	Appendix No 6. Order No 208		
Operation(al) Order(s)	1/22nd Bn. London Regt Order No 208	08/10/1918	08/10/1918
Miscellaneous	Schedule		
Miscellaneous	Appendix No 7. Order No 209.		
Operation(al) Order(s)	1/22nd Bn London Regt Order No 209	10/10/1918	10/10/1918
Miscellaneous	Appendix No. 9. Order No 210		
Operation(al) Order(s)	1/22nd Bn London Regt. Order No 210	11/10/1918	11/10/1918
Miscellaneous	Schedule		
Miscellaneous	Appendix No 10. Order No 212		
Operation(al) Order(s)	1/22nd Bn London Regt Order No 212	15/10/1918	15/10/1918
Miscellaneous	Appendix No. 11. Order No 213.		
Operation(al) Order(s)	1/22nd Bn London Regt Order No 213	13/10/1918	13/10/1918
Miscellaneous	Appendix 13. Order No 214.		
Operation(al) Order(s)	1/22nd Bn London Regt Order No. 214	16/10/1918	16/10/1918
Miscellaneous	Appendix No. 14. Order No 215		
Operation(al) Order(s)	1/22nd Bn London Regt Order No 215	17/10/1918	17/10/1918
Miscellaneous	Appendix No. 15. Order No 216		
Operation(al) Order(s)	Operation Order No. 216.	17/10/1918	17/10/1918
Miscellaneous	Reference map Sheet 36		
Miscellaneous	Appendix No 16 Order No 218.		
Operation(al) Order(s)	1/22nd Bn. The London Regiment Order No. 318	25/10/1918	25/10/1918
Miscellaneous	Appendix No 17. Order No. 220		
Miscellaneous	1/22nd Bn. The London Regt. (The Queens).	27/10/1918	27/10/1918

WO95/2732 (6)

Sept '18 – May '19

1/22 London R

47TH DIVISION
142ND INFY BDE

1-22ND LONDON REGT
~~MAR 1915~~-MAY 1919
SEPT 1918

47TH DIVISION
142ND INFY BDE

142/41

1/22 London R
Vol 2 8

June 1917

On His Majesty's Service.

Duplicate War Diary
3/1/16 to 30/4/16

D.A.G. Base

WAR DIARY or INTELLIGENCE SUMMARY

Army Form C. 2118.

1/22nd Bn Lon Regt

Vol 43

Place	Date	Hour	Summary of Events and Information	Remarks and references to Appendices
ADERLY WOOD	1/9/16		Battn remained in same position and received orders as to be possible. About 6.0 p.m. verbal orders were received that the Battn would be required to attack early next morning trench just East of BOUCHAVESNES MONASTER TRENCH with an objected MONASTER TRENCH in C.6.c and C.12.b. On receipt of these orders Battn was assembled by Coy in Valley near advanced Battn HQ. where Coy Commanders were given orders and the situation explained to them as far as possible. 2/Lt F. TROUNCE joined for duty. Battn moved forward to assembly positions at 12 midnight. Battn HQ established at C.13.a.1/2. Advanced Battn HQ at C.15.b.b.b.	
BOUCHAVESNES	2/9/16		Assembly was carried out in spite of great difficulties without a hitch and the Battn attacked at 5.30 a.m. in accordance with Orders No. that are known to Jerry on his first forming up. Strong opposition was met with and eventually heavy SOKROWITZ TRENCH running through C.5.d and C.5.b was taken as final objective. At 12 noon Capt. J.E. FLEMING M.G. and 6th Bn. later SOKROWITZ TRENCH with 2/Lt Bn. London Reft on left and a Company 1/22nd Batn London Reft Bn.T. up to reinforce on right. (Capt W.R. WHEELER with No 20 G. was in support in GERMAN WOOD TRENCH in C.10.b.	
			Casualties: Capt C.H. Oakley Died of wounds. 2/Lt J Bruce Killed. 2/Lt A. Hollier wounded 2/Lt J Innes " About 150 o.r. Killed, wounded, missing.	

WAR DIARY
INTELLIGENCE SUMMARY

Army Form C. 2118.

1/22nd Bn Lon Regt

Place	Date	Hour	Summary of Events and Information	Remarks and references to Appendices
WEST OF MOISLAINS	3/9/18		Information received from the Pioneers on our left that the enemy were withdrawing from their bank. 14th Inf Bde were instructed to push forward strong patrols and make good the line of the Canal Banks. Patrols from one Battn were pushed forward during the night to MONASTER TRENCH and from to Canal Bank through C.11a6 where connection was obtained with 47 Division on left and 22nd Bn. Gates Rgt on right. 2/Lt MAYES + COLESHILL Hos odr Jones the Battn from Deft. Day quiet on the whole and casualties slight. Chief difficulty experienced was carrying forward rations to the front line Companies. Lt Col Y.I. Paget's slightly wounded but remained at duty.	
CANAL BANK	4/9/18		Battn moved forward to SORROWITZ TRENCH about C.S & 60.25. Major O'Brien assumed Command of the Battalion. Lt Col Paget remaining at 142nd Inf Bde H.Q. Patrols crossed the Canal Bank early in the afternoon meeting with little opposition. At about 8.0pm a message was received from Brigade to the effect that Patrols were to be pushed forward from East from our front line to reach together running through D.8, D.H and D 20 b. Posts were to be established here and Patrols pushed forward to trench system in D.9 + D.15 so far as possible. Evening Orders received that 141st Inf Bde were to form though us early the following morning. Other patrols were accordingly pushed forward to D.8, but a later message received from Brigade cancelled the instructions for patrols forward of the line running North + South through D.I. Central. This was carried out. Enemy artillery very active in neighbourhood of MOISLAINS during the day. Our casualties slight. With the exception of forward posts all men were disposed in line along Canal Banks.	

Army Form C. 2118.

1/22 R. E Kent Regt

WAR DIARY
or
INTELLIGENCE SUMMARY.
(Erase heading not required.)

Place	Date	Hour	Summary of Events and Information	Remarks and references to Appendices
CANAL BANK	5/9/18		141st Inf Brigade attacked early in morning and for right secured for returning prisoners apparently offensive being directed. Msg. from Adjt (?) Division knows S.F. statics on line now as follows:- SIGNAL COPIE:- D.8.c.5.3,- D.20.a.9.5. 140th and 141st Inf Bns were to attack at 10 pm under arrangements to gain the line of trenches running North and South through D.9.b.1.b. and D.15.a. to known ridge at D.15.a.5. but thence S.W. along main road. At this time this 125 Division on our left were to attack NURLU. Has Inf Bn were to push and reorganise as far as practicable. Quiet night. 2/Lt. RENWELL M.C. & Lt. FRANK	
Do.	6/9/18		Orders received from Brigade at 2.0 am that 47th Division would continue the advance at 8.0 am that morning 140th Inf Bn on right and 141st Inf Bn on left 142nd Inf Bn following immediately in rear with 23rd and 24th Bns L.F. Regt in front and 22nd Bn London Regt in Support. 22nd Bn London Regt were to remain in present position and were not to move without direct orders from Bde H.Q. Commanding Officer saw all Coy Comdrs at Bn HQ at 7.0 am and explained the general scheme of the attack. 140 & 141st Inf Bns were to note that the known position passing through D.10 to D.16. 142nd Inf Bn would then pass through them taking LIERAMONT and Ship ground South of it. At 7.45 am information received that 12th Divn had not taken NURLU on previous night Artillery were therefore advised to fire immediately to gain touch with this up of 141st Inf Bn and conformed with them forming flank defence flank towards NURLU.	

Army Form C. 2118.

1/5₂ R. Lon. Regt

WAR DIARY
or
INTELLIGENCE SUMMARY.
(Erase heading not required)

Instructions regarding War Diaries and Intelligence Summaries are contained in F. S. Regs., Part II. and the Staff Manual respectively. Title pages will be prepared in manuscript.

Place	Date	Hour	Summary of Events and Information	Remarks and references to Appendices
	6/9/18 cont'd	9.0 am	The Officer Commanding 5th Berks (2nd Division) informs Major Bryan that he had received a message that NOREUIL had been captured by his Battn. His Coy's reported to Bryan's H.Q. and A. and B. Coys which were forming the defensive flank were to remain in their present position.	
		12 noon	Morning Orders received that the Battn would be relieved that night by 1st Bn. Cameron Regt. (5th Sp. Div. (Inf.)) and that the 42nd Sp. Div. would be pushing through 11th and 140th Inf. Bdes as frequently stated. Battn HQ relieved by 6 p.m. Coys relief in accordance with above orders, and on relief proceeded to area C.15 near BOUCHAVESNES for the night. Relief complete 3.0 am.	App. 1
BOUCHAVESNES	7/9/18		Battn moved by motor lorries from BOUCHAVESNES to CLERY SUR SOMME where it bivouaced for the night. Lieut Colonel Greenwood D.S.O., T.D. joined the Battn, and assumed command after six months tour of duty in England. App Lieut Colonel Greenwood CC/220.	App. 2
CLERY SUR SOMME	8/9/18		Battn in bivouac. Rain and very high winds prevailed during the night consequently the Battn spent an uncomfortable night. Battn moved by bus to MERICOURT L'ABBE after Orders No 2. Transport proceeded by march route in advance moving off at 6.0 am. Buses were late and did not move until 6.30 pm. Battn in Billets at MERICOURT at 11.30 pm. Very fine bright night, but no hostile bombing.	

Army Form C. 2118.

WAR DIARY
or
INTELLIGENCE SUMMARY.
(Erase heading not required.)

1/22 Bn Lon Regt

Place	Date	Hour	Summary of Events and Information	Remarks and references to Appendices
MERICOURT L'ABBE	9th Septr.		Battn in billets at Mericourt and rested during the day. In afternoon Battn moved by train to LILLERS area as per order No Z.1. Night spent in the train.	21/9/3
ECQUEDECQUES.	10th		Battn arrived at LILLERS STATION at 10 am and proceeded by route march to ECQUEDECQUES and billeted. Rain prevailed during journey. A very great difference was noticed in the Coln. Civilians had been evacuated to a great many of the billets badly bombed. The surrounding was totally different from what they were in Nov. Dec. 1915 when the 47th Divn was in this area. Battn in billets at Ecquedecques 10.15 am. Coy Commanders & men went round Inspectes and all Remainder of the day spent in cleaning, rectifying billets and putting.	
Do.	11th		Arrangements made for a Battn parade to Brice but owing to any heavy rain was partially indefinitely cancelled. Inspection of kit etc by Coy Comdrs carried in Billets gradually. Lewis gun staff attached to the Battn inspection rifles of the Battn and further all in working order.	
Do.	12th		Battn moved by route march to LOZINGHEM, as per order Divisional free heavily at commencement of journey but ceased soon after. Kit & mill Remainder of day spent in cleaning & fitting billets. Capt Maj. V. H. RABY proceeded on short leave to England.	

WAR DIARY.

1/2 R. W. Regt

PLACE		
LOZINGHEM.	13th	Battn in Billets and very comfortable. Battn drill for the AYCHET aerodrome parade during morning. Lewis gun, Scouting, Signalling and Stokes Gun specialist classes under Bn instructors. Evening on to make up establishment of Battn. 2/Lt. M. T. ALLEN] 1st Bn. London Regt. joined Battn for duty from Base. 2/Lt. J. BANNISTER] J. H-V. CASE
Do.	14th	9.0 am to 10.0 am Battn drill on aerodrome. Remainder of morning Coy. under Coy arrangements. Specialist classes carried on as yesterday. Lieut. H.S. DAVENPORT 22nd Bn London Regt. joined Battn from Base.
Do.	15th	Battn paraded Service C.E. in large hanger on aerodrome. Rev. CHASE C.F. conducting the service, and afterwards took passing operations by rites of high parade.
Do.	16th	Coy training on AYCHET aerodrome from 9.0am to 12.30 pm Specialist training carried on afternoon attention being paid to revision training for the Battn Football match at ALLOUAGNE. Clean clothing issued. C.O. inspected Bn. transport on aerodrome in afternoon. Battn Follies (BERMONDSEY BUTTERFLIES) gave performance in the evening, 2nd CCS. programme attached.	App.
Do.	17th	Battn lewis specialists paraded on aerodrome for examination twice during morning. On firing further trench on range at RAMBERT during morning. A Rifle field-on range at ALLOUAGNE in afternoon.

1/22nd R. Fus. Regt.

Place			
LOZINGHEM	17th (contd.)	Lewis Gun instruction at lecture when a machine gun in afternoon. Music lecture class before transport under Brigade Officer. Coys. waited their Baths whilst the Brigade was having arrangements made for Brigade Lecture Scheme in afternoon but afternoon cancelled. Drama Players in front of 22nd Bn. in evening. Remainder of Battn. bathed at ALLOUAGNE.	
Do.	18th	Battn. proceeded in motor lorries for evening exercises behind order Brien. Usual specialist classes. Officers and NCOs had a small lecture scheme arranged and supervised operated by the Battn. and a small landing scheme arranged and supervised. Recreation Room opened by the Chaplain Revd. Chase.	
Do.	19th	Battn. moved to CONTEVILLE area on account of there being too far from training stations other no. 201. Billets very poor and extremely bad. Only sufficient room for two thirds of Battn. application having 30 tents, only 15 previous arriving. By sympathy A & B Coys went into the huts and French aerodrome and left C and D Coys in tents the at BERTHONVAL. Battn. HQ. and Orderly Room Staff in CONTEVILLE village.	Apls 5
CONTEVILLE AND BERTHONVAL.	20	Coys. finished under Coy arrangements. Specialist training carried on particular attention being paid to Lewis Gun. Lecture to ITALY postponed for unknown reasons.	
Do.	21st	Commanding Officer inspected A & B Coys manoeuvre Coy. Coy. under Coy arrangements. Specialist training carried on. Coy. Officers moved from BERTHONVAL to CONTEVILLE aerodrome in afternoon. 2/Lt. Ed TERRY of 19th London Regt. joined Bn. for duty from France. 2/Lt. A A. PRINCE	

WAR DIARY

1/22 Bn 20 Regt

PLACE		
CONTEVILLE	22nd	Parade Service in hangar at aerodrome in morning. Rev. CHASE conducted the service. Capt. W.R. WHEELER proceeded on leave to England.
Do.	23rd	Batt. life in normal. Specialist training Carried on under specialist Commanding. Battn. sports being held on aerodrome in afternoon. Programme attended heather. Inclined to be wet. Tug of war sports went off well. 2/Lt. S.W. JARVIS returned from Corse of Instruction. Afft. to.
Do.	24th	Batt. life in aerodrome in morning. Special Lecture given to Offr. training Specialist training in usual Special Lecture given to Offrs. training this afte. by Pte. GYMKHANA held in aerodrome in afternoon. A very good afternoon and Competition from the Battn. its especially well Programme of events themselves attended. Offs. Jollification performance in evening. Weather quite good.
Do.	25th	Batt. life in aerodrome in morning, for one hour Specialist training as usual. Divine service in afternoon. Divine service of the Sacraments held in Cap. after Bn. Divine service of the Sacraments known.

D.S.O. Lt. Col. Lt. Pagold

Bar to M.M. 651941 Sergt. B. Lett. MM.
69336 J P J Pulley MM.
650905 J G Skelton M.

M.M. 650736 Pte W.A. Smith 629049 Pte Cordon Pl
694813 Pte Carver 694040 Ope Jeans Pte
654333 Pte J.C. Kennitt 694056 Pte St. Pierre Pte
650 575 J A Jones 694913 Pte Clint Stephenson
650 909 Ma on G Edwards 691278 Pte Ptsmonte
698 159 Pte R Southwood 698538 Pte Relmmeny D
698211 Pte G Pratt 698578 Pte G Manning D
698125 Pte J R Bryant 698137 J Pte Donaldson
698499 J R Bryagt J

M.C. B. LAMBERTH M.M. Lewis W. Patrick Hay Rose
Capt. G. COMER M.C. Trench Bn. Loudon'd Pte James Archer 2nd Lt. J. Davis |

1/22nd. Lon. Regt

WAR DIARY.

PLACE.	DATE.		
BONNEVILLE	26	Battn. paraded as ordinary [?] for ceremonial drive. Specialist training as usual. Particular attention being paid to Lewis Gun & German M.G.	
Do.	27	Bn. moved by march route to ST. PO--- (BONNEVILLE sub-area) and billeted in FRANCECOURT (Hq) PT HOUYIN (A Coy) ECOIVRES (C & D) Accommodation fairly good as Order No 202	App. 6
FRANCECOURT PT HOUYIN ECOIVRES.	28	Coy parades under Coy arrangements. Review of Coy training. Specialist classes held as before. German bellicose kilt A&B working together A&D C&D!	
Do.	29	C.O.E. Parade Service at FRANCECOURT at 9.30. R.C.'s to parish church. Parade at BONNEVILLE after church and in afternoon for A, B, D & Q Coys. Clean clothing inspection	
Do.	30	9am to 12.30pm A&B Coys and C&D Coy trained in their Coy areas. Coy trellis. Afternoon class held on pages for PT HOUYIN training with German machine guns. Demonstration was to be held in the use of Lewis Guns.	

6.7.H. Greenway
Lt Col
Comdg [?] 1/22nd Bn (The Queens)

2/10/18

Army Form C. 2118.

WAR DIARY
or
INTELLIGENCE SUMMARY.
(Erase heading not required.)

CONFIDENTIAL

WAR DIARY

1/22ND BN. THE LONDON REGT.
(THE QUEEN'S)

OCTOBER 1918.

IN THE FIELD.

WAR DIARY or INTELLIGENCE SUMMARY

Army Form C.

(Erase heading not required.)

Place	Date	Hour	Summary of Events and Information	Remarks and references to Appendices
FRANSECOURT ECOIVRES & ST. AUBYN	1/10/18		Bns in Billets.	
			Coy and Platoon training under Coy arrangements.	
			Specialist classes under Bns Hd qrs Instructors.	
HQ	2/10/18		Bn entrained to LA GORGUE AREA marching to ST POL where the entraining detrained at MERVILLE and marched to BULLS HANGARS as per orders No. 102	Appendix 1
			Accommodation under canvas	
LA GORGUE	3/10/18		Bn moved by march route to hide near PAVISSENT (Sheet 36 SW) and parked in the 4-30 pm as per order 204	Appendix 2
			whilst HQ and Coy Comdrs reconnoitred forward.	
			C.O. Adjt. and Coy Comdrs reconnoitred forward.	
			Bn moved to FROMELLES by march route as per orders No. 205	
FAUQUISSART			Bn in trenches Right Sector where they relieved the morning of 4/10/18	Appendix 3
FROMELLES	4/10/18		Bn hard march to assembly positions and Advanced in accordance with Orders to be able to take shelter in craters	Appendix 4
		4.2. C.S.Gs were fired during the night in places on PROMELLE and the British had to take shelter in craters	
		etc. Bn suffered no casualties before dawn.	
			Coy Comdrs then took over all Coy Orders at Bn HQ (N.23.a.52) at 0330 and approached the	
			West of the Advance	

WAR DIARY
or
INTELLIGENCE SUMMARY.
(Erase heading not required.)

Army Form C. 2118.

2nd Batt. R. Ir. Regt.

Place	Date	Hour	Summary of Events and Information	Remarks and references to Appendices
FROMELLES	4/10/18		Assembly accomplished at extremely sharp to reach previously allotted out at Le MAISNIL for distances of 3,000 yards and without casualties.	
			Major K.R. O'BRIEN (2nd in Comd.) deployed forward into (est. O.H. DB.R.I.C.7) (Sh.57) and established Advanced Battn H.Q. in farm building at O.13.d.2.6. (LE MAISNIL). Rear Battn H.Q. remained at FROMELLES.	
			At 06.40 Battn advanced in front other line East but met no opposition until nearing the Railway Embankment at BRAUNGHEM where they came under very heavy machine gun and rifle fire. A/Coy was (?) Coy frequently had to withdraw to line of A Coy on their left.	
			M/15 Battn Advance patrols held up by hostile gun fire. Artillery support to this however bombarded enough for advance and 10:30.	
			After the artillery support it was found impossible to advance further without protection by armoured cars. Many machine gun & rifle fire had increased stifling fire and he has slowly pushed back inconsolable and advanced posts established.	
			At Battn H.Q. line eventually the Battn O/(?) asked to O.22 a.5.5. for a 24 hour and right were filed in by Coys of 12/2018 and 15/18 respectively. After artillery cooperating increased ability in BEAUCAMPS.	
			Further very active. Heavy braid on Railway Embankment.	

WAR DIARY or INTELLIGENCE SUMMARY

Army Form C. 2118.

2/2nd Lon Regt

Place	Date	Hour	Summary of Events and Information	Remarks and references to Appendices
IN LINE	4/10/18		Orders received from 142nd Inf Bde in afternoon that no further advance was to be made	
			during the day. 140th Inf Bde was to pass through us and continue the advance	
		15.40	Situation unchanged and consolidation well in progress	
			Casualties:- OFFICERS: KILLED 2/Lt A.A. PRINCE. 2nd 2/Lt J. BANNISTER	
			WOUNDED 2/Lt H.Y. CASE and CAPT R.C. MAYES (since died of wounds)	
			OTHER RANKS. Killed 9 Wounded 38	
IN LINE	5/10/18		Patrols during night reported no movement by enemy	
			Enemy plane flew over low altitude over our lines this morning speared out apparently	
			enticed by the plane	
			Daylight patrolling carried out noting of not interest discovered	
			Instructions from Bde pursuant to the effect that in the event of an advance the Bn and	
			2/LILLE would not be retained by Bnptn. Operations were to take place North and	
			South with the entrances to the town frequent	
			Bn to be relieved by 1/23rd and 1/24th Battns in accordance with Bde No 207 and	Appen 5
			moved to LE MAISNIL. Battn fulfilled in Sultan Shafts's trench the immediate	
			counter attack Battalion	

(3)

Army Form C. 2118.

WAR DIARY
or
INTELLIGENCE SUMMARY.
(Erase heading not required.)

22nd [Bn?] The [...] Regt.

Instructions regarding War Diaries and Intelligence Summaries are contained in F. S. Regs., Part II, and the Staff Manual respectively. Title pages will be prepared in manuscript.

Place	Date	Hour	Summary of Events and Information	Remarks and references to Appendices
LE MAISNIL	6/10/18		B Coy carried back all their bodies to CHATEAU DE PLANQUES before relief. Casualties Nil.	
			Relief by HALLAMSHIRES completed	
			Anti aircraft guns mounted by Coy teams.	
			A empty British Lewis Gun Co. Commander recovered same.	
			Officer sent him into No Mans Land to retrieve as [it?] was not known [whose?] it was.	
			Scouts of 62nd DIV RELIEVED. Casualties Nil.	
do	7/10/18		[?] found vacated camp between all Coy Centres at 09.45	
			B Coy looked at night digging trenches in front area	
			Lt. W.G. HUMMER ordered [...] for [duty?] from down inspected to D Coy. Casualties Nil.	
do	8/10/18		Conf Officers from all Coy Centres at 12.45 and went round to reconnoitre lines	
			[...] 15.30 and returned [...] and that [...] held the line in [...] to ["A" Coy?]	
			Relief complete 22.05	Appendix 5
			Lt. C.C. SANFORD joined Battn tonight and posted to "A" Coy.	

WAR DIARY or INTELLIGENCE SUMMARY

Army Form C. 2118.

24th Bn. Lon. Regt.

Place	Date	Hour	Summary of Events and Information	Remarks and references to Appendices
FRONT LINE	9/10/18		Whole of 1st & 2nd lines 1/12 or and 1/Queen 1/30 or went out on the Battn front from 02.00 to 03.15 and from	
		03.00 to 05.00 respectively both with orders to establish themselves forward if the enemy had	
			evacuated — Machine guns were very active but superbly quiet. The second (and)	
			Battn patrol located enemy at approximately O.16.b.8.4 and consequently withdrew.	
			Situation generally — Quiet.	
			Casualties. Nil.	
			Lt. T.H. BARRON joined the Battn for duty and posted to "A" Coy.	
	10/10/18		Patrol of 1 Sgt & 8 O.R. went out at 0001 Frelinck 02.00 No enemy encountered but very heavy	
			machine gun and rifle fire from entrenchments met when trying to cut the 2nd belt of wire.	
			Enemy wire found to be very strong.	
			Patrol of 1 Officer and 11 O.R. went out at 02.00 to 04.00 they also encountered very heavy machine	
			gun fire active about 200 yds from the Entrenchment. Enemy exceedingly alert	
			Very light were fired from Enemy's Entrenchment. Capt. W.R. WHEELER rejoined from leave.	
			Capt (T/Maj) V.M. BABY returned from leave.	
			Lt. J.F. PRESTON M.C. (7th London Rgt) joined the Bn. for duty posted to C Coy	
			Casualties. 1 O.R. killed in Action.	

Army Form C. 2118.

WAR DIARY
or
INTELLIGENCE SUMMARY.
(Erase heading not required.)

1/5th R. War. Regt.

Instructions regarding War Diaries and Intelligence Summaries are contained in F.S. Regs., Part II. and the Staff Manual respectively. Title pages will be prepared in manuscript.

Place	Date	Hour	Summary of Events and Information	Remarks and references to Appendices
FRONT LINE	11/10/18		4th Battn. carried out small patrols on enemy positions & Railway Embankment below	Appendix 7
			Orders No 209 Reft attached	Appendix 8
			No identification obtained	
			Casualties returned attd	
			Enemy troops all heavy	
			Enemy more tends to be very strong and in strong defence	
			Battn relieved by 1/6th Bn. Ridg. Regt. and moved to LE MESNIL in accordance with Order No 210	Appendix 9
			Casualties Nil	
LE MESNIL	12/10/18		Battn. in Brigade Reserve Resting and cleaning	
			2 days in old German Intermediate Camp and 2 in bivouac shelters and trenches	
			Capt. WEAVER, McKENNON Bothn. & Lieut Aston b. mother on England posted to "B" Coy	
			Casualties Nil	
Do	13/10/18		Battn. at PROYELLE attended to the Brigade at United Battn. hatted	
			In evening & during the night LE MESNIL was shelled heavily with H.E. and Gas shells.	
			Respirators right but no casualties	
			Following appointments take effect from to-day:—	

Army Form C. 2118.

WAR DIARY
or
INTELLIGENCE SUMMARY.
(Erase heading not required.)

12 R. Ir. Rgt.

Instructions regarding War Diaries and Intelligence Summaries are contained in F. S. Regs., Part II. and the Staff Manual respectively. Title pages will be prepared in manuscript.

Place	Date	Hour	Summary of Events and Information	Remarks and references to Appendices
LE MAISNIL	12/10/14 (con'd)		Lieut. T.A. BARROW appointed 2nd in Command "A" Coy	
			2/Lieut. J.A. POOLEY transferred from "C" to "B" Coy & appointed 2nd in Com'd. Coy	
			Lieut. J.F. PRESTON M.C. appointed 2nd in Command "C" Coy	
			2/Lieut. S.W. JARVIS transferred from "A" to "D" Coy & appointed 2nd in C.D. Coy	
			Capt. F. WEAVER M.C. to Command "B" Coy	
			Orders received from 24th Bde by Batn at about 21.00 that from various indications it was known that the enemy had withdrawn opposite the Brigade front. 24th Batn were therefore carrying out a reconnaissance in force in early hours of 14th during which Reserve Coy (D) to this direction.	
			Order was received to "D" Coy to move up and occupy the positions vacated by 1/9th Batn in D.11. a Letters known on 14th work. This Coy was then placed under orders of 15th Batn London Regt.	
			Casualties Nil.	
LE MAISNIL	14/10/14		Search & escalater carried out by 1st Batn London Regt. apparently proved from the enemy was still very much in evidence.	
			"D" Coy was gradually released that night and returned to its old Billets in the	

WAR DIARY
or
INTELLIGENCE SUMMARY.

(Erase heading not required.)

Army Form C. 2118.

2/4th Lon Regt.

Place	Date	Hour	Summary of Events and Information	Remarks and references to Appendices
			Returned to Camp.	
LE MAISNIL	15/10/18		Major General Sir C.J. Cuninge (Div Comdg) visited the Camp.	
			Bn. ordered at 02.00 by Bde from Division that the enemy had been ordered on his invaders front, also to be ready to withdraw from in front of the line.	
			Same having returned from Bde. train at 08.00 that the enemy had withdrawn on the Brigade front, the 1/23rd Bn were resting in Tents with him and 17th Div. Regt. "A" (instructions to the Adjutant) would come into force forthwith.	
			Bn. was then ordered to stand to the prepared to move at 10 minutes notice.	
			Conveying Officer and Adjutant proceeded to CHAU DE FLANDRES at 08.00 hours to meet Maj. Pipkins General.	
			Bn. was moved to positions at 8.14 a.m. at 10.00	
			Advance of 1/23rd Bn was apparently about. Withdraw from opposition being unopposed	
			At 12.30 Orders were received to move from Camp and another bn. restore attached to concentrate in grounds of Chau DE FLANDRES with a view to move forward through 1/23rd Bn with 1/24th Bn.	
			At 14.30 this concentration was complete.	

WAR DIARY or INTELLIGENCE SUMMARY

Army Form C. 2118.

...R... Regt.

Place	Date	Hour	Summary of Events and Information	Remarks and references to Appendices
			Order No 212 was issued	Appendix 10
			Coys began forward to assembly positions on Embankments with 1/4 E Bn's on right	
			A position reached at 16:15 that 1/23rd Bn had not reached as an advance to line	
			before attack brought about the attack by 1/23rd & that Bn was accordingly	
			deferred for that day	
			Coys remained in their assembly positions	
			Cookers etc were moved up to CHAU DE FLANDRE and MG Coy sent up to Coy	
			Battn HQ remained at CHAU DE PROVIDE	
			At 21:30 orders were received from 103 Inf Bde that the advance would be continued	
			at 05:15 following day by 1/23rd and 1st Battns under cover of an artillery barrage	Appendix 11
			their Bde to Objectives here given. His Bde are being line of Canal Bank	
			Order No 213 was issued at 23:00 to this effect	
			Major E.W. MAYBERY MC joined Battn for duty	
			Casualties NIL	
16/10/18			Battn passed through 1/23rd Bn at 05:15 Objectives shown on attached map	Appendix 12
1st Line			Battn to march at 06:00 am to Railway Embankment at	

WAR DIARY or INTELLIGENCE SUMMARY

Army Form C. 2118.

Place	Date	Hour	Summary of Events and Information	Remarks and references to Appendices
IN LINE			Report received from Capt H.R. Whistler (O.C. B Coy) at 06.00 stating first objective gained with slight opposition in Trench north of the Pin de la Guerre & his right. C Coy on his left.	
			Batt. HQ moved to PIN DE LA GUERRE at 09.00	
			O.C. B Coy reported that they were held up by machine gun fire and the advance was delayed.	
			At 11.00 orders were sent to O.C. A Coy to send two platoons to sweep trenches East of FORT ENGLOS (which had previously been reported clear of the enemy by Patrols) thus attacking the Batta frontage and enabling us to push forward the advance on the left and thus enabling the right flank of the advance to get forward.	
			These platoons met with some machine gun and artillery fire but by 17.00 "A" Coy was established on its left flank firing ammunition through P.L.C.	
			C & D Coys had also moved forward but had established posts and found hand patrols active & were in touch with the enemy.	
			At close of day the Battn was disposed:—	
			"A", "C" and "D" Coys in front line	
			B Coy in Reserve.	
			Casualties nil of O.R.	

Army Form C. 2118.

WAR DIARY
or
INTELLIGENCE SUMMARY.
(Erase heading not required.)

02 A/ion Regt

Place	Date	Hour	Summary of Events and Information	Remarks and references to Appendices
IN LINE	16/10/18 (cont)		During the night some patrols were sent out. There were very difficult by enemy machine gun fire and artillery fire which held entrenched until about	
		02:00	The enemy evidently pulling himself of everything ammunition before evacuating his positions	
Do.	17/10/18		At dawn about fifty prisoners were afterwards sent out. They reported that the enemy had apparently from here considerably during the early hours of the morning and that the country was clear of the enemy to a line running North and South through D.2.c. Central.	
		09:30	2/5 and 2/7 King's Own fine Regiment passed through the Batten in advance with other Bn 214	Appendix 13
			Battn withdrew to LE MAISNIL where they had dinner and afterwards entrained at PROMELLES and proceeded by light Railway to FOSSE area where orders to 215 Support moved by road in advance	Appendix 14
			Billets in area were very indifferent, Battn remained the night there. Camilles Hu.	

Army Form C. 2118.

WAR DIARY
or
INTELLIGENCE SUMMARY.
(Erase heading not required.)

Instructions regarding War Diaries and Intelligence Summaries are contained in F. S. Regs., Part II. and the Staff Manual respectively. Title pages will be prepared in manuscript.

Place	Date	Hour	Summary of Events and Information	Remarks and references to Appendices
FOSSE	18/10/18		Batten moved by route march to BOURECQ in accordance with Order No 216	Appendix 15
			The march although long was carried out by all ranks in good style and no one fell out.	
			Casualties NIL	
BOURECQ	19/10/18		Batten in Billets at BOURECQ.	
			Day devoted to cleaning up & fitting &c	
			Commanding Officer Assumes Command at 1400, and takes over the general direction	
			Sunday	
do	20/10/18		C of E parade service at 10.30 in field at N.W. of Village. Officers attended	
			R.C. and Non-conformist Services in Village. Church Parades inspected by	
			O.C. and have contained Officers and Warrant Officers and Sergeants of the Battn.	
			Prizes presented to the Winners to the Battn. Inter Platoon letc	
			Battle at MONT-EN-ARTOIS allotted to the Battn.	
			Classes in Musketry, Lewis Gun, Scouting, Bombing, Gas Guard allowed Battn Instructors	
			C.O. Visits training areas Co. Co. Headquarters	
do	20/10/18		Billets Searched at 08.45 by those Commands twice	
			Greatest Cleanliness insisted upon by Batt. Parades	
			A Coy sends party to S.T.R.M.	

Army Form C. 2118.

WAR DIARY
or
INTELLIGENCE SUMMARY.
(Erase heading not required.)

Place	Date	Hour	Summary of Events and Information	Remarks and references to Appendices
			Platoon and Company training remainder of day.	
			Instructions received from Bde that Major EN WATHEN was to command "A" Coy	
			vice Major PARKER until 6 "A" Coy & Capt ST ELMONT be reassumed Coy 2nd in Cmd	
BOURECQ	23/10/16		Batln paraded at 08.45 for 1 hour Ceremonial drill.	
			Specialist Classes as usual after Bn parade.	
			Stokes Mortar range at T.M.'s	Cont. firing free fuses pattern demonstrated started by 1/2nth Ca Regt illustrating the latest formations & methods of attack which had proved to be successful in recent operations undertaken by this Divn
			Platoon and Company training remainder of morning	
BOURECQ	24/10/16		Batln paraded at 08.45 for 1 hour Ceremonial drill.	
			Specialist Classes as usual after Bn parade.	
			B.M.'s And bn broadly participated in bomb throwing 10.45	
			Platoon & Company training in the Coy areas	
			2/Lt E L GARDINER (who returned back from Base Nov 17th to "B" Coy	
			Monthly Signalling Musketry Games (etc) under Battn Instructors	
BOURECQ	25/10/16		Battn parade for presentation of DCM ribbons by Major General Sir	
			G. Smyth (Divnl Cmdr), following members of this Battalion were	
			invested :—	

WAR DIARY
or
INTELLIGENCE SUMMARY.
(Erase heading not required.)

Army Form C. 2118.

Place	Date	Hour	Summary of Events and Information	Remarks and references to Appendices
BOURLON	27/10/18		M.C. Capt. J.G. Gleming, Lt. McDade	
			D.C.M. R/Sm. Th. Bain, Sgt. R. Butler	
			2nd Lt. May Mellow, 9/Brocompton	
			M.M. Lt. A. Davis, Lt. J. Watson, Sgt. J. Jones, Cpl. Seer, Alex. Moore, Pte. Pyle	
			Pte. Bennison, Pte. Cook, Pte. Lyle, Pte. A. Jones, Pte. Gordon, Pte. Jenkins	
			Pte. Smith (L.A.), Pte. McInnes	
			Information has recently been received in running that reinforcements have arrived	
			the line. Lt. Enderson & Pte. Clark & Corp. Bu Coulle Jremented these pillars-elders	
			have no other.	
			A/Col. MacDonald came the Divisional Commander attended the Battalion and	
			stated that the work it had done during the previous 3 months have	
			especially in the Many Performance on 22nd August 1918.	
			Battalion Mood to por K N this as p. order No 217	
BOURLON	28/10/18		Night working around outposts, relief coming off the line steadily time	Appendix 16
			was no fixing pointe.	
			Battalion in billets at 19.30 hours	

Army Form C. 2118.

WAR DIARY
or
INTELLIGENCE SUMMARY.
(Erase heading not required.)

Instructions regarding War Diaries and Intelligence Summaries are contained in F. S. Regs., Part II. and the Staff Manual respectively. Title pages will be prepared in manuscript.

Place	Date	Hour	Summary of Events and Information	Remarks and references to Appendices
LOOS	20/10/16		Prior to return to civil practice were unable to arrange for Battalion to welcome them individually, somewhat however took [place] at the intermediate receiving station (where) the Divisional General (General Armstrong) gave a short address to each of the Battalion, as it returned to the Armoured Billets (?) and — which we had observed in clothing hitherto, not before [foot?] [?] — [?] people held dry [?] and [?] as the Battalion marched through to places of AUCHOUREN and LOOS. Others were in tears when the Queen's Band had stopped playing in the square in addition they failed to march through but apparently elected for the uncomfortable return [route] to Battalion to Billets.	
LOOS	21/10/16		Day spent in [handing] and [drawing] equipment etc. A C.g. was [detailed] as [Advance] C.g. to [?] from the Armoured [?] to take [?] to take place on 23rd inst. O.C. "A" Coy had the S.O.I.A.M. [?] [?] in [?] at 14.00 to receive full instructions as to the [?] his C.g. were to take in the next day ceremony.	

Place	Date	Hour	Summary of Events and Information	Remarks and references to Appendices
Loos	25/9/18		The Battle of Loos phase 1st git at the absence from the enemy and lasted no time with the Germans not understood.	
			The Battalion under Major LITTLE as part of the 47th Division on the morning of the opening day of the 5th Army Commander's explained in Order No 220 and moved into position.	Appendix 17
			We were received with great enthusiasm and cheering by the inhabitants, who lined the roads and filled the windows and balconies. In truly British fashion we marched though at "attention" which prevented our troops retrieving the feelings of the populace to known they were had been. The faces of the people showed signs of suffering, anxiety and depression of spirits. The chefs - especially parisian chefs - accidentally empty. The people were here elated. Returned of the troops was a sparkling of spirits billing which has given special leave advance able to book before the relatives after French troops are of years. As an experience it was certainly unique but the spectacle effect was rather hindered by the fact that owing to orders from higher authority the

16.

WAR DIARY
or
INTELLIGENCE SUMMARY.
(Erase heading not required.)

Army Form C. 2118.

22 B Bn/Sy/

Place	Date	Hour	Summary of Events and Information	Remarks and references to Appendices
HELLEMMES	29/10/18		Guns and rifle had now not allowed to fire. The men in places stood talking although infantrymen were also slightly improving. Also from the Army Commander and to have pillars in the hands places the Battn marched to billets in HELLEMMES which comparatively speaking was a suburb of the healthy city. Men were in "close" billets being clustered over a large area. Both bands on parade. Were being of friends found in the neighbourhood, much ceremonial drill practised as the Brigadier General had arrangements in intention of inspecting the Brigade the next day. The City of Lille was known even to our British troops.	
Do.	30/10/18		The Brigadier General inspected the 3 Infantry Battalions of the Brigade. The inspection conducted with a much gusto. Company Platoon training left home.	
Do.	31/10/18		In evening Sir Jellico gave a performance in large eating down to Poke HR	

G.W. Grimwood
Lt Col
Comdg. 22nd B. (B.W. Rey.)

SECRET.   Copy. No 2

        1/22nd Bn The London Regt Order No 203.

                                                2nd Oct. 1918
                              today

1. 1/22nd Bn Lon Regt will move by march route to ST. POL and thence
    by train to LESTREM LA GORGUE AREA.

2. Lt. Darlot will act as entraining Officer. H.Q. C and D Coys
    will be in position in column of route on the ST POL - NUNCQ road
    at FRAMECOURT at 7.45 am. Coys will move off at intervals of
    100 yards.

3. A and B Coys will be in position in column of route at the
    Railway level crossing across the ST POL - NUNCQ ROAD at 7;50 am.
    They will join the Battn in rear of D Coy.

4. Billetting party of 2/Lt. Bannester and C.Q.M.Ss. of A., C. and
    D Coys will report at Bn H.Q. at 7.30 am.

5. All blankets, Officers valises, mess boxes etc to be dumped at
    Coy H.Q. at 7.30 am. One man per Coy will be left in charge

6. O.C. Coys will see that their billets are left in a clean and
    sanitary condition.

7. Battn H.Q. will close at FRAMECOURT at 7.30 am and reopen on
    arival in new area.

    DRESS - FULL MARCHING ORDER.

                                          2/Lt & A/Adjt.
                                    1/22nd Bn The London Regt.

    Copy 1 Filed.
         2 War Diary.
         3 O.C. "A" Coy.
         4   "B"
         5   "C"
         6   "D"
         7   H.Q.
         8 Q.M.
         9 Adjt.
        10 2nd in Comd.
        11 R.S.M.
        12 M.O.

Appendix N° 2.

Order N° 204.

SECRET   Copy No. V

1/22nd Bn The London Regt Order No 204.

Ref Sheet 36A.   3 10 18.

1. Battn will move by march route to RUE TILLELOY today 3rd inst and be in Support to 141st Inf Bde, in order H.Q., A, B, C, D Coys. 100 yards distance will be maintained between Coys.
   ROUTE. Road through L 36 a and b - L 36 a - RUE DE PUITS to H 22 b 9 5 - thence along Winchester Road to RUE TILLELOY.
   Assemble along line of RUE TILLELOY from junction with Winchester Road to road junction N 13 c 1 9.
   Coys will be in position in column of route on road running past H.Q. facing South. First Coy will move off at 7.30 a.m.

2. Dress - Fighting Order. ~~xxxxxxxxxxxxxxxxxxxxxxxxxxxxxxxxx~~
   ~~xxxxx~~. Cardigans will be carried. Packs and blankets will be stacked at Coy H.Q. and collected later by Q.M.

3. Depots and Horse Lines will be prepared to move forward at short notice.

4. The following will accompany the Battalion:-
   Cookers, Water Carts, Mobile Reserve, Tool Carts & Pack Animals with pack saddles.

5. Company Commanders will be mounted.

                                         [signature]

                                         2nd Lt. & A/Adjt.,
                                         1/22nd Bn The London Regt. (The Queens).

No. 1 - File.
    2   War Diary.
    3   Second in Command.
    4   M.O.
    5   T.O.
    6   Q.M.
    7   O.C. H.Q. Coy.
    8   "A" Coy.
    9   "B" :
   10   "C" :
   11   "D" :
   12   R.S.M.

Army Form C. 2118.

WAR DIARY
or
INTELLIGENCE SUMMARY.
(Erase heading not required.)

CONFIDENTIAL.

C.G. 39.

WAR DIARY

1/22ND BN. THE LONDON REGT.

NOVEMBER 1918.

Place	Date	Hour	Summary of Events and Information	Remarks and references to Appendices

WAR DIARY or INTELLIGENCE SUMMARY

Army Form C. 2118.

Place	Date	Hour	Summary of Events and Information	Remarks and references to Appendices
HELLEMMES	1/11/18		Batt. moved by route march to WILLEMS AREA, and billeted at RUE FRANCAIS as per ORDER No 221	APPENDIX 1
			Coy arrived at billets receiving new parties.	
			Roll in billets 1400 hrs.	
			Billets fairly comfortable.	
RUE FRANCAIS	2/11/18		Coys and Battn. + HQ parades. Cleaned up.	
			Signalling and scouting classes carried out under Batt. Instructors.	
			Batt. was visited by two Hundred Journalists / Swiss and Dutch conducted by	
			Officers from 5th Army Intelligence. They spoke to the boys with the Batt. being	
			paraded attention to be inspection and coming afterwards.	
			In the afternoon of the Pictures Shews were sent advanced to Lille	
			and another returns of the Pictures Shews were freely at the Mens	
			Assembly Rooms has not been to Divisional Cinemas and Sing Song (impromptu) at the dest	
RUE FRANCAIS	3/11/18		Brigade parade Services C.B. Divisional Concerts (both from Sing Song (impromptu) at the dest	
			From the premises that the Hundred LO receives J. Military hon	
			605059 Capt. J.H.A. HILES. "A" Coy 61224 Hop R.A. PARRATT "B" Coy	
			61653 Pte E JACKSON "A"	
			Sergt. J. C. MORGAN "A"	

Army Form C. 2118.

WAR DIARY
or
INTELLIGENCE SUMMARY.
(Erase heading not required.)

Instructions regarding War Diaries and Intelligence Summaries are contained in F. S. Regs., Part II. and the Staff Manual respectively. Title pages will be prepared in manuscript.

Place	Date	Hour	Summary of Events and Information	Remarks and references to Appendices
IN FRANCE	1/1/19		Col. and Adjutant handed over to Corporal arrangements	
			Signing and leaving Charge under Battalion Instructor	
			4 officers and 120 or how 25th Surrey Rifles joined the Bn. for instruction	
			Battalion being attached to "A" Company and to "C" Company and the Cyclist headquarters	
			"B" Company. They received at our metropolitan arrivals as the training area	
			contained both Belgian towns and inhabitants difficulty over the language question	
			resulted in their reception being quite enthusiastic	
			The rather left no complete platoons and none tried to be exactly the same	
			lines and side by side to the men. Billets Rooms	
			Coy. and Platoon Orderly Rooms. Company Offices.	
			Standing and Special changes under Battalion Scheme.	
			Received Information that trade line work with a view to handed to training	
			on account of the Thaw.	
IN FRANCE	2/1/19		Information received that following decorations awarded to this Battn.	
			MILITARY CROSS. Major K.B. OREEN (17th Lond. Regt.)	
			Lieutis. C.W. PARRY. G.S.	
			FRENCH MEDAILLE MILITAIRE. Lo: ostas	

WAR DIARY
or
INTELLIGENCE SUMMARY.
(Erase heading not required.)

Army Form C. 2118.

Place	Date	Hour	Summary of Events and Information	Remarks and references to Appendices
RUE FRANCAIS	6/11/18		Battalion prepared to move at night.	
			Orders cancelled owing to very heavy rain.	
			Orders were given allotting to Battn. certain personnel cancelled.	
			Officers and 3 Other Ranks per Bn from Res. on exchange for Canadian troops to be sent to England for the time of duty.	
RUE FRANCAIS	7/11/18		Battn. billets at TRESPLOUVE (some marching troops)	
			Battn. moved to forward line at the and behind the Bn pos. Res. as per ORDER No 222. appx R.	
			Allied advance rapidly in heavy enemy shelling en route. Enemy rearguard actions with M.Gs. H.Ms during night. 108 Bde Battalion Portuguese proceeded to line with the Battalion.	
			Casualties Lt. T.H. BARRON wounded	
			1 O.R. killed	
			2 O.R. wounded	
			1 Portuguese missing afterwards returned.	
FRONT LINE	8/11/18		Detachment of Royal Engineers were employed on repairing and recutting Battn HQ.	Appendix 3.Y
			Inhabitants of the Defensive advanced areas	
			Rumours again reported that enemy was withdrawing on their front. They seemed close	

Army Form C. 2118.

WAR DIARY
or
INTELLIGENCE SUMMARY.
(Erase heading not required.)

Instructions regarding War Diaries and Intelligence Summaries are contained in F. S. Regs., Part II. and the Staff Manual respectively. Title pages will be prepared in manuscript.

Place	Date	Hour	Summary of Events and Information	Remarks and references to Appendices
FRONT LINE			Situation on our front.	
			The bridge over the river had been subject 2 Army previously to attack footing down the river.	
			Owing to hard rains it seemed that the construction of a new bridge would be an operation of very difficult character.	
			Orders from A.1 Officer were SO or Supplies to 520th Siege Coy RE this nights to carry up the necessary bridging material as in view of the general situation it was considered imperative that a bridge should be put across the river that night.	
			Enemy machine guns and sporadic shooting active up to midnight.	
			Casualties NIL.	
FRONT LINE	9/11/18	05:00	Lt. WAKEFIELD 520th Cv RE's had completed bridge across river about 100 yds South of PONT-A-CHIN. Details have sent across at once and discovered that the enemy had evacuated during the last 2 hours.	
			Instructions for the OFFENSIVE were put into force at once.	
			The whole Battn was across the river by 08:30.	
			A section of 11th Corps Cyclists were attached to the Battn for purposes of ...	

(A9175) Wt: W3353/P3361 600,000 12/17 D. D. & L. Sch. 51a- Forms/C2118/15.

WAR DIARY or INTELLIGENCE SUMMARY

Army Form C. 2118.

Place	Date	Hour	Summary of Events and Information	Remarks and references to Appendices
			The Battalion marched from pre-arranged with the Battn.	
			First aid Scouts & Stretcher-bearers were found in "B" Coy (the leading Coy) occupied MONT ST AUBERT at 08.20 with C Coy on their right and "A" and "D" Coys in Support just EAST of HAVRON — TOURNAI Railway. At 09.30 instructions were received from Brigade HQ that MOURCOURT was to be made good. "B" and "C" Coys occupied MOURCOURT with no opposition. Left Bois Fort. Ent. Dist at 14.50 hours. Battn then moved to RAIN at 12.00 and thence to BIZENCOURT at 15.00. No armed opposition was met. Battn was met with enthusiastic receptions by the Civil popu. At the close of day the Battalion was disposed as under:— 2 Coys MOURCOURT. 2 Coys and Battn HQ BIZENCOURT. Rations were brought up at night under great difficulty as the enemy had completely blown up main road. Orders received at 21.30 that the Battn would be orders the following day at 4-hours.	

WAR DIARY or INTELLIGENCE SUMMARY

Army Form C. 2118.

(Erase heading not required.)

Instructions regarding War Diaries and Intelligence Summaries are contained in F. S. Regs., Part II. and the Staff Manual respectively. Title pages will be prepared in manuscript.

Place	Date	Hour	Summary of Events and Information	Remarks and references to Appendices
ADVANCING			3rd Inf Bde acting as Advance Guard to the Division. Inner objective given. Line L.29 central L.29 central L.35 central. Covekts No.	
ADVANCING	10/11/18	07.00	Batn. took up at 07.00 hours in Brigade with Orders to C.9.34 with 1/230	Appendix "A"
			Bon. forder Ruff on the left. A Coy leading to vanguard.	
			No opposition was encountered but at 10.30 hours an advanced line was	
			established by A' & B D Coy Hdqtrs L.29.b. not at A' Coy being	
			in touch with 9th Division on right at Montrequet L.35 b.c.1. B and	
			C Coys. and Batn. H.Q. were at HACQUIGNES. but at 14.00 when new pairs were	
			for the whole of the Battn. to move to MOUSTIER. On no one complained by	
	16.00		The reactions of the Balko were again of the most enthusiastic nature	
			It was evident that the people of this neighbourhood had spent perilous in	
			the hands of the enemy having the pole 4 years. Several instances of	
			very great brutality were brought to our notice of the country.	
			Batn. HQ bivouacs in proximity to tent erected on the cricke in all avenue	
			Refer to the annexure of movements of the men.	

WAR DIARY or INTELLIGENCE SUMMARY

Army Form C. 2118.

Place	Date	Hour	Summary of Events and Information	Remarks and references to Appendices
MOUSTIERS.	10/11/18		Orders received at 02.00 that Bdy Hqrs would move back each empty lorries in Bizencourt. Men were used under the Offr i/c Cg.	Appendix 5
			On being the ARMISTICE the men all wrote letters home. (I wrote my letter of last moments in case of Krs.	
			any. Not the Batt. HQ in a hut apart from Bttle.	
			On arrival in BIZENCOURT it was found that Bttle would not appear to arrive until the 12th. Batts. and offrs invited to the side of the road to know time C Coy and Bn HQ moved on further 2 mile out	
			Allotted Kensselia in BOURGAGE. A billeting party sent to the town.	
BIZENCOURT & BOURGAGE	11/11/18		Return to Billets. All troops given Pte to Cpl inspection etc which had been changed in last areas were attended to (arms and kit etc fires)	
D.O.	12/11/18		Battalion moved to Billets in LA TOMBEE in ourzemen markets No 55. Bttn in Billets at 15.00 hrs. Biths were very comfortable	Appendix 6

WAR DIARY
or
INTELLIGENCE SUMMARY.
(Erase heading not required.)

Army Form C. 2118.

Place	Date	Hour	Summary of Events and Information	Remarks and references to Appendices
LATOMBE	12/4/18		Parties in Billets as for Jourba.	
			Orders received for Bath returns by the Chaplains (Rev. W. Clegg) now the Company	
			Officer. He letters went on the resuscitation of the work done by the Battn. during	
			the 23 days remaining in France and congratulated all ranks on their part in	
			saving the line. He was to make no official conclusions to which in these times	
			the difficult periods in front of Maison to deliver themselves & the more	
			attributable to men that they h.d done during the period of active fighting	
			The Officer and 130 rank of the 25th Portuguese Bgte left in the morning after	
			having been attached Coys. 16 of 4th inch show coming had been looked forward	
			to with mild curiosity by their personal friends in France were not	
			on the whole were also a considerable attraction & difficulty in finding where in an	
			unknown tongue to convey orders to them. Volunteerers made themselves	
			understood of the speakers, Captain's opinion was, back in billets into an	
			active alliance. Live difficulties remained at ease - the language	
			question was solved by their friends. & these Portuguese was quite good	
			and and for the previous for which they have seldom fires are packed.	

WAR DIARY
or
INTELLIGENCE SUMMARY.

(Erase heading not required.)

Army Form C. 2118.

Place	Date	Hour	Summary of Events and Information	Remarks and references to Appendices
	14/1/19		Yesterday the ultimatum known and respects to levant, RA at once adopted an attitude of strong hostility and their insulting and frequent discipline marred foot. When one platoon with 10th African soldiers were indifferent and unsympathetic with mutinous spirit.	
LA TOMBE	15/1/19		Battn. to Bulito	
			Battn. moved by road to CYSOING (WILLS AREA) in our lorries with others.	Appendix 7
			Billets exceptionally good and comfortable.	
CYSOING	16/1/19		Battn. in Billets.	
			Capt. French at 10.30 for three Iwana studies.	
			4 trench motor the spare officer.	
			Interesting lecture from Rev. H.A. on a member of the Battn. to 2/Lt. Pte. JACK HARVEY "A" Coy has won the Victoria Cross. References relating thereto definitely to Gallant conduct is attached. The Commander Officer proceeded to pillow on the Battln. Parade.	Appendix 8

WAR DIARY or INTELLIGENCE SUMMARY

Army Form C. 2118.

(Erase heading not required.)

Place	Date	Hour	Summary of Events and Information	Remarks and references to Appendices
ONSONG	17/11/18		Batts in Billets at Onsong.	
			Church of England Church Service in Cinema at 10.15 hours.	
			Roman Catholics to Coln at 09.30	
			Roman Catholics to local Church at 09.00	
			New Communion in Cinema at 12.00	
			Evensong H.K.C. in Cinema at 12.30.	
Do.	18/11/18		Batts in Billets at Onsong	
			Coy Comd and Platoon Training 09.00 to 12.00 under Coy arrangements	
			Post Headquarters & other posts were inspected by Snrs for Adj.	
			Lectures [illegible] Signal Offrs	
Do.	19/11/18		Battn in Billets at Onsong.	
			Coy and Platoon training 09.00 – 12.00 under Coy arrangements	
			Athletic Finals in the Drill Shed	
			Court of Enquiry held at the Bn of Gatras Battn Licensed Stores	
			The following Offrs [illegible] the Battalion for duty and were posted to Coys as OC's against their names	

WAR DIARY
or
INTELLIGENCE SUMMARY.

(Erase heading not required.)

Army Form C. 2118.

Instructions regarding War Diaries and Intelligence Summaries are contained in F. S. Regs., Part II. and the Staff Manual respectively. Title pages will be prepared in manuscript.

Place	Date	Hour	Summary of Events and Information	Remarks and references to Appendices
			2/Lt E. GERRARD "D" Coy	
			2/Lt R.J. LEACH "A" Coy	
			2/Lt A.T. GREEN "C" Coy	
			2/Lt B. LANGWORTH M.M. transferred from "D" Coy to "B" Coy	
			Divisional Pigeon officer under to arrangements of the Chaplains Daily paper	
			machine gun training continued supplies	
			C.O. Coaching own horses. Church parade 2/Lt J.F. PRESTON M.C. to	
			take over from the Brigade Curve Coaching show	
			Divisional Golbie performed in these Church at the Ration at 17.30 - A.	
			Left flanks by C.O.B. performance	
			Both in Bubble & Squeak	
			Tf and station dinner 09.00 - 13.00	
			Afterwards tennis about three	
			Arrangements were for a Rifle Contest in Old Factory tomorrow to the Stage	
			& not being quite ready, the contest had to be postponed	
ALSOU G 30/6/12			A further practice Cross Country was have place.	

WAR DIARY
or
INTELLIGENCE SUMMARY.
(Erase heading not required.)

Army Form C. 2118.

Instructions regarding War Diaries and Intelligence Summaries are contained in F. S. Regs., Part II. and the Staff Manual respectively. Title pages will be prepared in manuscript.

Place	Date	Hour	Summary of Events and Information	Remarks and references to Appendices
OSSING	20/1/19		Battn. Billets at [illegible]	
			Companies out at station game under Coy arrangements	
			Woollen undies dealt [illegible]	
			Classes of the [illegible] illiterates naters in the Battn. now were commenced	
			under the Chaplain and Mr N.C. Plummer. Only those men	where knowledge of
			[illegible] reading writing was very poor attended. Strength [illegible] about 50 men	[illegible]
			the Commandant Divs inspected the [illegible]	
			[illegible] was [illegible] from 10.30 [illegible] Mr [illegible] A. Sutton R.C.	
			[illegible] Colonel here [illegible] given. The Division has completed the	
			[illegible] allotment [illegible] part of the [illegible] for everyone. No [illegible] was arranged	
			by the Div Maine. Battn. Orchestra played for the first time.	
			[illegible] was [illegible] cool but the [illegible] given to the orchestra [illegible] was warm + enthusiastic	
D.O.	21/1/19		Battn. in billets as [illegible]	
			Protestant Parade 07:30 - 10:30 Divine Service	
			Coy. [illegible] and [illegible] [illegible] under Company arrangements	
			[illegible] wrote the [illegible] this	

Army Form C. 2118.

WAR DIARY
or
INTELLIGENCE SUMMARY.
(Erase heading not required.)

Place	Date	Hour	Summary of Events and Information	Remarks and references to Appendices
CASSING			Yeomanry Ret eating dinner served out December Ration	
			Consecrated for members 1/c S.B. Preston as usual.	
Do	25/12/18		Parton to Pilité	
			Battalion parade in Battle Dress formed 09:30–10:30 Dinners attended	
			Coy Platoon Sergts. Irregular order Coy movements 10:30 to 12:45	
			Riflemen under if own officers	
			Elementary fd artilley class carried on as usual	
			Jewish Service in Synagogue & field every facility given to Jews	
			members of the Battalion to attend.	
			The following officers joined for duty Rank & Regt transferred to Bn stated	
			Capt R.M. EWEN (Queens R.W.S. Regt) A Coy	
			Lieut S.B. SHANNON M.C. (7Bn W.R.) C Coy	
			Lieut C.G. KING M.C. (11/3 W.R.) B Coy	
			2/Lieut TYSOE (15 W.R.) C Coy	
			Lieut A. ROTHLAY (2 W.R.) B Coy	
			2/Lt J Motley transferred from B to D Coy	

WAR DIARY
or
INTELLIGENCE SUMMARY.
(Erase heading not required.)

Army Form C. 2118.

Place	Date	Hour	Summary of Events and Information	Remarks and references to Appendices
			Route to Cross Country run to place at 14.30. 40 members of the Battn took part.	
			Draft reinforcements arrived from Base Details Depôt.	Appendix 9
			Draft reinforcements arrived from M.G. Training unfortunately too young had	
			been sent to collect them from Base but unfortunately they had	
			gone up to instruments arrived and there proved no further.	
SOING	24/11/18		Bn in Billets at Cysoing	
			Church of England Church Service in Cinema at 09.15	
			Army Commanders at 10.00 whole Room	
			Roman Catholic service in C of E Church at 10.00	
			Voluntary Celebration of Holy Communion Cinema 10.00	
			Cinema at 10.30	
			Commanding Officer and 2 Lts Smith & Atherton attended Thanksgiving Service in the local Catholic Church both Perfecture Civique and Staff and Commander in Chief 23rd and 24th Battns	
			Raining Battn received to the Battn to move to the Lieu area, billeting party under A/W.O. Parker proceeded to HAUBOURDIN which will be the station area	

WAR DIARY or INTELLIGENCE SUMMARY.

Army Form C. 2118.

(Erase heading not required.)

Place	Date	Hour	Summary of Events and Information	Remarks and references to Appendices
GODING	25/11/18		Battalion by route marche to HOUBOURDIN (the first stage of journey) in accordance with	APPEN 10.
			Order No 117.	
			The Brass band headed the Battalion en route to put people seeing "VERDETTE"	
			Battalion in Billets 2.30 p.m.	
			Billets were not very comfortable due to there being a large extent	
HOUBOURDIN	26/11/18		Battalion resumed the march & travelled to BETHUNE (the second stage of journey) in	APPEN 11.
			accordance with Order No 118	
			(over 20 miles)	
			The march was a very tiring one. Several Halts were accomplished along the way.	
			made to rest the men but only rode. Battalion arrived about 5.15 p.m. Billeted in	
			the Old Cavalry Barracks which had suffered rather badly from the Boche	
			shelling during the Summer. Battn HQ now in Chateau which has been	
			vacated by General Dupuis a few miles N. Bethune	
BETHUNE	27/11/18		Battn again resumed the march and proceeded to ECQUEDECQUES (the final stage)	APPEN 12.
			in accordance with Order No 119	
			On arrival in Ecquedecques it was found though some billeting parties	
			had been made work. It is to arrange keeps that Billets had	

Army Form C. 2118.

WAR DIARY
or
INTELLIGENCE SUMMARY.
(Erase heading not required.)

Instructions regarding War Diaries and Intelligence Summaries are contained in F. S. Regs., Part II. and the Staff Manual respectively. Title pages will be prepared in manuscript.

Place	Date	Hour	Summary of Events and Information	Remarks and references to Appendices
ECQUEDECQUES	25/11/18		Isn relieved the Portuguese Battn as we were to demobilise and once more the front-nowhere in extent with our advance Allies and the time in every way was less friendly however. No situation briefly became a little confused and was only cleared by the untiring efforts of the English area officer attached to the Portuguese Battn who succeeded in keeping everybody in better accord with the staff concerned requests, where in removing billets to both Bathers in a most impartial manner while the time maintaining the most rapid conversation in both lan[guages]. Portuguese Battn moved out of Village, thus giving the Battn the whole of the Village to billet in. Billets were arranged & the Battn was fairly comfortable. Coys with independent etc.	
Do.	26/11/18		Battn in Billets at Ecquedecques. Coy training including Shapnees, Close Order Drill & Decentralised games which Colonel arranged. Arrangements made with School Master for Schoolroom to be used as Battn Recreation Room. Piano practically without trouble.	

(A9150) Wt W2358/P363 500,000 12/17 D. D. & L. Sch. 53a. Forms/C2118/15.

Army Form C. 2118.

WAR DIARY
or
INTELLIGENCE SUMMARY.
(Erase heading not required.)

Instructions regarding War Diaries and Intelligence Summaries are contained in F. S. Regs., Part II. and the Staff Manual respectively. Title pages will be prepared in manuscript.

Place	Date	Hour	Summary of Events and Information	Remarks and references to Appendices
BONNEVILLES	30/11/18		Bois Rullier.	
			Coy & Platoon training to include Bayonets & Bivouacs &c.	
			Baths north of Bethune.	
			Repairs tramps under Repair officer.	
			Classes in Elementary Education in School room under the Chaplain.	
			Recreation Room opened 12.00 to 21.00.	

C.T. Brunger
Capt. & Aut
Comdy 123rd Bn Canadian Railway Troops
(The Durango)

(A9175) Wt W3138/P360 600,000 12/17 D. D. & L. Sch. 52a. Forms/C2118/15.

Army Form C. 2118.

WAR DIARY
or
INTELLIGENCE SUMMARY.
(Erase heading not required.)

WAR DIARY.

1/22nd Bn LONDON REGT.

DECEMBER 1918.

CONFIDENTIAL.

Army Form C. 2118.

WAR DIARY
or
INTELLIGENCE SUMMARY.
(Erase heading not required.)

Instructions regarding War Diaries and Intelligence Summaries are contained in F. S. Regs., Part II. and the Staff Manual respectively. Title pages will be prepared in manuscript.

Place	Date	Hour	Summary of Events and Information	Remarks and references to Appendices
ESQUELBECQ.	1/1/18		Church of England Parade service in Y.M.C.A tent. fellow, Drums and Band attended.	
			Rev. Chase conducted the service.	
			Celebration of Holy Communion immediately after Parade Service.	
			Roman Catholic Service in Cinema on Esquelbecq.	
			Rest. Stores and Night's Training taken for amusement.	
			Films in Cinematograph. Education held in Schoolroom under the Chaplains	
			in Charge of those all ranks of the Battn its three Education Standards (a) Elementary	
			(b) average (c) advanced. It was decided to held an examination thoughtout the Battn.	
		2/1/18	the Education Officers acting as Invigilators. From this examination men were	
			picked and placed in the respective grades referred to above.	
			A Coy have expended this day	
			in order to select the Boxers team for the Brigade Boxing Competition	
			which was being held in the near future. Shields alts, per Coy, needs to	
			the Divisional knife for Practice	
			Revl Ashman Joined for Duty and posted to "B" Coy.	

Army Form C. 2118.

WAR DIARY
or
INTELLIGENCE SUMMARY.
(Erase heading not required.)

Instructions regarding War Diaries and Intelligence Summaries are contained in F. S. Regs., Part II. and the Staff Manual respectively. Title pages will be prepared in manuscript.

Place	Date	Hour	Summary of Events and Information	Remarks and references to Appendices
ECQUEDECQUES	3/10/18		Coy Platoon and specialist training 0900 to 12.00 under Coy arrangements	
			Range at 13.30 p.m. (100 yards) allotted to C Coy	
			Elementary education at 11.30 in Schoolroom	
			"B" Coy examined for Lading Proficiency	
			Coys carrying from in afternoon under Lt. Col. Preston M.C.	
Do.	4/10/18		Coy Platoon and specialist training 09.00 to 12.00 under Coy arrangements	
			Div. Comdr (Major General Sir C.L. Farringe) presented V.C. ribbon to Private Jack Harvey in Attendance at 11.45 Parade consisted of representative levies of each Battn in the Brigade. "A" Coy represented this Battn.	
			Div Commander heartily congratulated the recipient on his well deserved honour	
			Brigade Shooting Competition at Allouagne Range opened. One Lewis Gun Section detailed for coming competition	
			Elementary Education Class at 11.30	
			"C" Coy examined for grading purposes	
Do.	5/10/18		Coy Platoon and Specialist training under Coy arrangements 09.00 – 12.00 Elementary Education Class	
			Nos. 2, 5, 11 & 14 Platoons competed for the Daily Telegraph Shooting Competition	

WAR DIARY or INTELLIGENCE SUMMARY

Army Form C. 2118.

Place	Date	Hour	Summary of Events and Information	Remarks and references to Appendices
E COEUR DECQUES			Firing completed from 4 mins rapid followed by 10 rounds S.A.A. fired at silhouettes target at 200 yards. Results of the competition:	
			1st 1/22nd Bn London Regt 58 points	
			2nd 24th Bn London Regt 50 points	
			3rd 1/22nd Bn London Regt 47 points (No 2 Platoon)	
			Rapid & snap shooting bt Sgums Major James 24/L 2nd Lyman Major James 23/L 3rd Cpl Powell 24/L	
			1 Rapid 1st Major E. Whaythorn with 29 points.	
Do.	6/9/16		Company, Platoon and Physical training under Company arrangements	
			Elementary education class at 11.30	
			D Coy were apponted for fatigue in Layard	
			Stripe party of 1 [H.A.] Gunn and 32 other ranks for Armoury Rings in connection with Shooting Competitions	
			Congratulations to the Bris to convey Competition to Range	
			Lieut. W. R. WHEELER M.C. and Lieut. F. WEAVER M.C. who quitted their acting ranks of Capt. & Censing to Command Coys.	
			Capt. W.M. HAYTHORNTHWAITE joined the Bttn for duty & posted to "B" Coy to Command.	

Army Form C. 2118.

WAR DIARY
or
INTELLIGENCE SUMMARY.
(Erase heading not required.)

Place	Date	Hour	Summary of Events and Information	Remarks and references to Appendices
ECQUEDECQUES				
	1/1/18		Capt. A.F. BOTHWAY transferred from B to D Coy to command	
			Intensive attack in billets	
			Company Platoon & Specialist training continued. Coy arrangements	
			in view of Brigade Boxing Competition to be held in the New Year it was decided to give intensive Competition early training. Competition finalists passed under	
			2/Lt. H.T. ALLEN during the morning for training purposes	
			B Coy were examined in an elementary final for ranking purposes	
			3 NCOs were selected to represent the Batt. in the Lakes Bakers Working Comp.	
			Major Crosthwaite M.C.	2/Lt. R.A. Banks Som.
			Lieut. Perry	Lieut. Whitfield
			2/Lt. Morris	2/Lt. [illegible]
			Own [illegible] James	2/Lt. [illegible] Brown
			Result:	
			1st. 1/12 Bn. [London] Regt.	166 [points]
			2nd. 1/21 Bn. [London] Regt.	161 "
			[illegible] Bn. [illegible] Regt.	5[?] "
			[illegible] [illegible] Regt.	146 "

WAR DIARY
or
INTELLIGENCE SUMMARY.
(Erase heading not required.)

Army Form C. 2118.

Place	Date	Hour	Summary of Events and Information	Remarks and references to Appendices
ECQUEDECQUES			Wished several for Battn were as follows:-	
			Capt Ferrar Pds	
			2nd Lt Jenner 81	
			" Parsons 86	
			" Bush NCR '15	
			Sergt File MM 91	
			Adjm Lt Maybee MC 81	
			S. Matthews 76	
			Sjt Rose 65	
Do	8/12/18		Church service held in Ecquedecques fields 10.00 Divine Parade attended	
			Celebration of Holy Communion immediately after. Parade service 1st Chaplain latter at 0730	
			Commandant to School von BURBURE at 10.00	
			Roman Catholics in ECQUEDECQUES Church at 11.15	
			Cleaning in Schoolroom at 17.30.	
			Major Eric Mayhew MC was this Officer of Btn often aeroplane at BRUGES	
			completion MLOAGNE	

WAR DIARY or INTELLIGENCE SUMMARY

Army Form C. 2118.

(Erase heading not required.)

Place	Date	Hour	Summary of Events and Information	Remarks and references to Appendices
RAMSKERQUES			NCO's Rehearsal of Brigade Sports Officers & Other & Shooting Competitions	
			Held Lewis Guns and Competitions	
			Several Orders received for Brigade re Instructions of B.P.I. from R McDonell	
			from the Brigade to Commn. Base Dept.	
			Captn. Keough & Dottrar, returns visits R.M.C. at Yolen Resnel. Lieut 3th Row 2 gh.	
Do.	9/10/19		Company Platoon Officers had Training 9am to 12.00.	
			16 Coy were Ready in U. 26.0.0	
			Remedial Education class in Schoolroom at 11.30.	
			Boxing Competition Karrier instr by Lt. Allen.	
			Examination of A&B Coys completed	
			Voluntary Holland class assembled in Schoolroom at 11.30 under Lt Oxley. STOKES	
			25 Men attended	
			Total amount subscribed by the Battn to the Red Cross FUND was 1086 francs	
			Cross country Run in afternoon under Lt Sheehan Irvine.	
10/10/18			Coy Platoon and Specialist Training under Coy arrangements 0900 - 12.00	
			Ring in U.26.c. nearly "A" Coy	

Army Form C. 2118.

WAR DIARY
or
INTELLIGENCE SUMMARY.
(Erase heading not required.)

Place	Date	Hour	Summary of Events and Information	Remarks and references to Appendices
PROVIDEQUES			Orders issued the clothing and kits of the Bathn. being packed in the Square	
			Kitchen inspected	
			Band having an Olgos into McAllen	
			Lieutenant Schwitzer Chas. under Chaplain at 11.30	
			Commander of W. James in D Coy employed	
			in afternoon softball matches was Engr between the Bathn team and RAE on	
			letters from RAE won by 3-1 goals. 4 miners demobilized	
			Kilpatrick presents that Lt. Brown was awarded M.C. (now known as later)	
Do	12/3/19		Coy Platoon Specialist training	
			Rangs allotted to B Coy	
			Basin turned as usual	
			Elementary education class in School at 11.30	
			Lieut. Pope posted for duty & attd to B Coy	
			" Luff " " " A "
Do	13/3/19		8 NWFFO dismissed off	
			Coy Platoon Specialist training	
			Revd attd to A Coy	

WAR DIARY or INTELLIGENCE SUMMARY

Army Form C. 2118.

Place	Date	Hour	Summary of Events and Information	Remarks and references to Appendices
			Ongoing training under 2/Lt Allen.	
			Elementary Education.	
			Lewis platoon returned to Coy.	
Proven	14/7/18		Rev. allotted to "C" Coy.	
			B Coy marched to Reveillon Camp near the Battn.	
			in Support to rebuild and Practice road 7.45 a.m. left at 07.00 and 11.45	
			respectively. On arrival they were given	
			(7) were more fully familiarity with dispersal of the Battn to take these	
			positions to and from the Camp.	
			Lt G. Bourke Jerome is Truck had lichen 1.30	
			Celebration of Holy Communion immediately after C of E parade	
			Voluntary service in Schoolroom at 17.30	
15/7/18			N Conformists Parade at 10.00	
			Roman Catholic to Parish Church at 11.00	
			6 Coy supplied working party of 25 O.R. for work on Dwellings Camp being	
			conveyed by lorry at 09.00 returning 12.00.	

WAR DIARY
INTELLIGENCE SUMMARY
(Erase heading not required.)

Army Form C. 2118.

Place	Date	Hour	Summary of Events and Information	Remarks and references to Appendices
캠프듀크	6/1/19		Coy Orders issued giving under day arrangements. Elementary education class. [unreadable] instructors Methods class. Boxing competition [unreadable] under the Allied Purchasing Competition of C Coy proceeded to the Reveillon Camp. Purchasing 2 Platoons of C Coy previously occupied by C Coy clean clothing supplied. Latter baths given in Reveillon Camp Working parties each of 25 sorters in Reveillon Camp. Telegraphic message [unreadable] received from Her Majesty the Queen. "Many thanks for the kind wishes for the New Year, pray convey to the men and the officers my and the London Regt (The Queens) her sincere thanks for their good wishes for Xmas and the New Year, which Her Majesty most heartily reciprocates." signed EDWARD WALLINGTON	
Do.	17/1/19		The Brigade Commander inspected the Battn on parade on the Sortais Groun near Parade Ground at ALLOUAGNE at 10.00 Battn left Experience at 9.00 "C" before the Battn at ALLOUAGNE. The Battn was inspected in line and afterwards marched past in columns and quarter columns.	

(A9175) Wt W2353/P361 50,000 12/17 D. D. & L. Sch. 52a. Forms/C2118/15.

WAR DIARY
or
INTELLIGENCE SUMMARY

Army Form C. 2118.

Place	Date	Hour	Summary of Events and Information	Remarks and references to Appendices
Becordel	18/5/18		The Brigade Commander congratulates the remaining few on the state of the Batt. and wished all ranks to be informed.	
			Afternoon bathing done in Wodecourt at 17.30.	
			Nominations for Rifle Shot 68340 Serjt. E.J. Stokes awarded M.M.	
			Lew Platoon and Section training under Arrangements 09.00 – 12.00	
			Elementary musketry class at 11.30.	
			Notes compiled handed under Mr Allen.	
			Baths at Fricourt allotted to the Batt. class altered applied	
			Snow working parties 1/45 also provided to the Australian km & supplies by "B" Coy	
		11.30	Lecture & Instructional training under best arrangements 09.00 – 12.00	
B	19/5/18		Platoons and Specialist training under B in Schonburn.	
			Kit Inspection at 11.30	
			Church service at Aliceltre t & Indiching at 17.30	
			Planting class in Agriculture in	
			Special conf the trust as usual	
			Baths at Fricourt allotted to "B" Coy	
			2 working parties each 1/45 at Fricourt for work on Reference Crossing (front Somme) Det.	
			football match at Bresne in afternoon 12nd Ry v '23 pdr Bn 12nd I Batta. winning	

Army Form C. 2118.

WAR DIARY
or
INTELLIGENCE SUMMARY.
(Erase heading not required.)

Instructions regarding War Diaries and Intelligence Summaries are contained in F. S. Regs., Part II. and the Staff Manual respectively. Title pages will be prepared in manuscript.

Place	Date	Hour	Summary of Events and Information	Remarks and references to Appendices
E.Andrecque	30/12/17		Inf Capt R. Nil.	
			Rev flatrn specialist training under arrangements.	
			Christmas choir service at 11.30.	
			No training parties owing to Christmas day.	
			Boxing Competition in continuation with the Band held at Filleus Theatre at 17.30. Programme attached. An evening force highly amusing & successful.	≠
	31/12/17		Few from "C" Coy at Derullies were conveyed by lorries.	
D			Rev platoon and specialist training under Coy arrangements 09.00 to 12.00.	
			Christian education in Coat at 11.30.	
			Owing to the large amount of clerical work caused by demobilisation and Coy runners filling up the places from it no parade necessary to reinforce the Orderly Room staff with several clerks and also a separate Office. (One men of "A" Coy were completed under Battn arrangements.	
			Lots of Inter Platoon matches of the Battn Inter Platoon Competition were played off.	

WAR DIARY
or
INTELLIGENCE SUMMARY.
(Erase heading not required.)

Army Form C. 2118.

Place	Date	Hour	Summary of Events and Information	Remarks and references to Appendices
Edinburgh	22/7/16		Church of England parade service in Green Park Area at 11.00. Celebration Holy Communion at 11.30 in YMCA Hut.	
			Job meeting in boardroom at 17.30.	
			Communicants at Brotton at 10.00.	
			Relaxation in Saints Church at 11.00.	
			Saw little more given the Battn. by M.T. Corps. Film for the Cinema. during the afternoon. 2 officers 118 OR. for Coy & Bn. attended.	
			Coy Kitchen Specialist training under Coy arrangements 09.00 - 12.00.	
	23/7/16		Elementary Education Class 11.30.	
			Wearing distinct dress at 17.30.	
			AF2 to completed for "B" Coy with latter manoeuvres.	
			One Coy drummer sent to Colford by Nondispatch ??? to the amusement of the Comic staff and musician of the Battn. The staff had been extremely busy for 3 weeks & at last effected an apparently excellent ??? & there was a Guard Batt. Concert amidst a number of the Band ??? at Tileco Theatre at 17.30. Another successful evening & furnace studio.	

WAR DIARY
or
INTELLIGENCE SUMMARY.
(Erase heading not required.)

Army Form C. 2118.

Place	Date	Hour	Summary of Events and Information	Remarks and references to Appendices
Gaydeyra	24/12/15		Day spent chiefly in getting Regl. Dining rooms ready for Xmas festivities. A, Z & D Coys employed under Batta. arrangements.	
	25/12/15		**CHRISTMAS DAY** Mounted celebration Holy Communion 08.00 and 12.00. Dismounted celebration Geographic Church at 08.30 and 10.00. Christmas Service received for troops in Cinema at "A" Div Camp. Bnd played for matinee Coy Carols and B.& C.Sqns E.O.V. Hamilton Lessons & the "Queens". Morning occupied in decorating and furnishing the Rotundrooms and colonnades for the Xmas dinner. Leaf been their dinners at about 16.00. "B" Coy in the Rotundrooms, "A'D" Coy and Transport Section in Cinema attenuals. "C" Coy at Pavilion Camp. All leaf fed extraordinarily well of pork, turkey, Xmas pud. Pat, Xmas pudding etc. and much beer and rum. "A" Coy again soared over this live turkey centrepieces by Ptnor, it being obviously conviving that this fork has never eaten alive. He people being that it was refused by some very smelling turkeys.	

Army Form C. 2118.

WAR DIARY
or
INTELLIGENCE SUMMARY.
(Erase heading not required.)

Place	Date	Hour	Summary of Events and Information	Remarks and references to Appendices
Aug-Dieppe			The Village was comparatively quiet at 23.00. took the appearance of the Village returned in the early morning of the 26th and was some cases at any rate there was an entirely evening state of affairs	
Do	26/10/18		Day quiet and reconnoitering and manual pledge noting. Our Bois. staff held their drives in an elaborate Quring the opening there was much reference to a certain horse known as the "Pilot".	
Do	27/10/18		10.00 - 12.00 Ldy [Loy?] [?] especially training under bay arrangement Elementary education Voluntary class in Agriculture Machining	
			27.16 A.C. RM completed move to Burgement An official took his men into his slight knowledge of man, was necessary by the spectacle of demobilization of our troops. [?] turned loose on the Europe	
	28/10/18.		09.00 - 12.00 Foot Drills, Physical training Dying to mount. Elementary education [signature] James M Doolty	

Army Form C. 2118.

WAR DIARY
or
INTELLIGENCE SUMMARY.
(Erase heading not required.)

Place	Date	Hour	Summary of Events and Information	Remarks and references to Appendices
Bermuda	30/6/18		Lt E Baptiseau & others at 10.30	
			N.C.O.'s in Schoolroom Bustin at 10.00	
			R.E. in Bastine Chest at 69.00	
			Vol. courses in Schoolroom at 17.30	
	31/6/18	09.00–12.00	Col Slater Specialist training under Coy arrangements	
			Elementary Education as usual	
			Band as usual	
		17.00	Col. Shattock class at 17.00	
		18.00	Col. Class in Elementary Physics at 18.00	
			M.O. inspected all men of A Coy. The examination was requested by higher authority into a view to ascertaining any men especially the young recruits were suffering from any complaint & the best means to the recent severe epidemic and if so to correct same by means of special instruction and attention. Special note for the majority of N.C.O. and men were inclined to [illegible] so into the refresher army after the war. The response was not enthusiastic	

Army Form C. 2118.

WAR DIARY
or
INTELLIGENCE SUMMARY.
(Erase heading not required.)

Instructions regarding War Diaries and Intelligence Summaries are contained in F. S. Regs., Part II. and the Staff Manual respectively. Title pages will be prepared in manuscript.

Place	Date	Hour	Summary of Events and Information	Remarks and references to Appendices
Gillingham	31/12/18		The unit paraded strong 3 offs and 9 men	
		6.00 – 12.00	Usual training	
			Dry run the roads at U He or	
			Kit brothers clean	
			Kit Inspection clean	
			Men examined in use of "B" bag	
			No unusual enemy activities	

(F. H. Simmons)
Lieut. Col.
Comd 1/22 London Regt. (The Queens)

4/1/19

Army Form C. 2118.

WAR DIARY
or
INTELLIGENCE SUMMARY.
(Erase heading not required.)

1/32 London
Vol 47

Place	Date	Hour	Summary of Events and Information	Remarks and references to Appendices
GR	1/1/19		Company Orders issued.	
Equedecques			Allotted to "D" Company.	
			Uniforms & underclothing were of B Company — object of employment	
Lillers			boys to search methodically every place especially those	
			assigned to his Company would rely on being aware of any	
			light from the right to leave or be house	
			Lieut. Nebb. Davies chosen as Clothing and Bootsman	
			"Examined R at 18.00 hrs". He has been	
			Riflemen at 18.00. & Liaison out to be	
		assigned to the		
	2/1/19		Phones to the	
			Behaved as if in order. Lieut. M.C. D. Luggage	
			Lilla offering scheme all with of 4.30 inspected	

Army Form C. 2118.

WAR DIARY
or
INTELLIGENCE SUMMARY.
(Erase heading not required.)

Instructions regarding War Diaries and Intelligence Summaries are contained in F. S. Regs., Part II. and the Staff Manual respectively. Title pages will be prepared in manuscript.

Place	Date	Hour	Summary of Events and Information	Remarks and references to Appendices
Equidocque	3/1/19		Company and Platoon training. Recreational games.	
" "			Elementary Education Class. Voluntary Bookkeeping?	
Lillers			Studied Class in the evening.	
			Battalion Competition for Bugles. Brass Band etc. having under	
			2nd Lieut Lerch. R.I.	
			Medical Officer inspected all men of transport and drew.	
			Regimental Observership of rifles detailed from this day.	
			In field Sheet 4. Inst on the left hand upper corner	
			Corrin the name and rank of the writer.	
			Handed in departure :—	
			Captain W.H. Raby	
			2nd Lieut L.W. Brown	
			" " E.J. Downley.	
			699241 Sergeant	
			"Bermondsey Buttaflies" gave a performance in LILLERS Theatre.	
			200 men provided on Demolition.	

WAR DIARY or INTELLIGENCE SUMMARY.

Army Form C. 2118.

(Erase heading not required.)

Instructions regarding War Diaries and Intelligence Summaries are contained in F. S. Regs., Part II. and the Staff Manual respectively. Title pages will be prepared in manuscript.

Place	Date	Hour	Summary of Events and Information	Remarks and references to Appendices
	4/1/19		Company Elementary Education class. Company under 2nd Lieut. R.J. Spears.	
			"Sport". Concert party of 5th Field Ambulance gave a highly successful performance at KIKKERS Theatre.	
	5/1/19		Church of England Parade – arrived whn C.O. the KIKKERS at 10.30 hrs. Roman Catholic ECQUEDECQUES Church Parade BERBURE CHURCH 10-30. Inter-Company Battalion football form. Games in the afternoon. 7/B.	
		11.00	Capt. W.B.Stray M.C. It was announced his appt. as Adjutant had been revoked at his own request. Company training Elementary Education class. Voluntary training etc.	
	6/1/19		Standard & Physical Boxing under 2nd Lt. Leech. Refresher. Has been received of the undermentioned award. 695092 Pte. Ball W.E. D.C.M. The award was made while previously but owing to the Battalion moving from the 1st Army the information was not communicated two men proceeded on Demobilisation.	

Army Form C. 2118.

WAR DIARY
or
INTELLIGENCE SUMMARY.
(Erase heading not required.)

Instructions regarding War Diaries and Intelligence
Summaries are contained in F. S. Regs., Part II.
and the Staff Manual respectively. Title pages
will be prepared in manuscript.

Place	Date	Hour	Summary of Events and Information	Remarks and references to Appendices
	7/1/19		Company and specialist training under Company arrangements. Range at U26a allotted to B Company. Boxing competition training under 2nd Lt R.L. Leach. Elementary Education class.	
	8/1/19		Voluntary Shorthand & Bookkeeping classes. Baths at IZZERS for all men of the Battalion. Company and Platoon training. Elementary Education class. Range at U26a allotted to D Company. D received days lie at Albuquae. Battalion allotted 142 and Lewis Guns. Battery by 3-1. Comparative essay match.	
	9/1/19		Company and specialist training. Range at U26a allotted Physical and Bookkeeping Voluntary Education classes. Boxing competition training under 2nd Lt R.L. Leach.	
	10/1/19		Battalion route march of approximately 6 miles concluding with a lecture from Medical Officer at IZZERS? Subject - Venereal Diseases. He succeeded in evoking	

(A9173) Wt W4356/P361 60,000 12/7 D. D. & L. Sch. 52a. Form/C2118/15.

Army Form C. 2118.

WAR DIARY
or
INTELLIGENCE SUMMARY.
(Erase heading not required.)

Place	Date	Hour	Summary of Events and Information	Remarks and references to Appendices
	10/1/19		This subject (in which he appeared to be an enthusiast) interesting and instructive, showing by means of the propaganda common well used of enemy & friends known only to our Allies of the Stars and Stripes. Four men proceeded on Demobilisation.	
	11/1/19		Company, Platoon & Specialist training. Range allotted to B Company. Superintendent Education class. Brigade Boxing Competition held in TESTER Theatre a thoroughly successful meeting. Winners from this Battalion were 68013 Pte Gibson J. span 18039 Pte Allen V. Winners Leather. Band of the 23rd Battalion supplied.	
	12/1/19		Inter unit panoramas on Demobilisation. Church of England parade-service in YMCA but ESTRÉES at 11.15. Chaplain of 23rd Battalion, conducted the service & Preached a forceful sermon. Roman Catholic service at ECQUEDECQUES proceeded on Demobilisation. Church 11.00. Ten men proceeded on Demobilisation.	

WAR DIARY
or
INTELLIGENCE SUMMARY.
(Erase heading not required.)

Army Form C. 2118.

Place	Date	Hour	Summary of Events and Information	Remarks and references to Appendices
	13/4/17		Battalion route march under Captain at Batbay - two companies	
			about Elementary Execution Also Helmet Education in	
			Physics - Shetland. Last advance on Demolition by	
			the Commanding Officer in Division. Start at 11:30. The	
			arrival despatched by road route in this grid comprising	
			report was invaluable. These grid-added for Demolition	
			Brigade work and Battalion ramed about 180 Strong.	
			2 Cookers and all available transport accompanied the	
			Battalion. Starting point passed at 10:45. Weather was	
			very anxious to find sprinto. Dinner was eaten at 7.6.	
	14/4/17		REVIEW: Camp. The Battalion marched and some direct	
			the new place with which it had been ordered to stop daily	
			in the course of the next few days. After dinner men	
			were marched up to Allenryn Football ground to watch	
			2nd Battalion of Roy. the 2nd Battalion in the Division to which	
			the 1st Bn. was assigned play in a match at the slaughter	

WAR DIARY or INTELLIGENCE SUMMARY

Place	Date	Hour	Summary of Events and Information	Remarks and references to Appendices
Zonnebeke	14/1/19		Out and about in our new area by 2/5 and we have now proceeded on Demobilisation lines.	
Lillois	15/1/19		Company's Platoon & Specialist training. Orders received for the move to B.W.E.F. Rest Camps on the 19th inst. Packing of stores generally the objective.	
	16/1/19		Temperatures taken and measured down to Zero Fahr. Situation changed suddenly for a prepared Divisional exam scheme, received order 2.15 PM. Forward for Area Comdr. was forced to have to part & notify Coy. of 180 troops to posts to hold and accept the circuit was KITKB3 Metre. The audience judged the show by some so that proper in the form of performance lightships lot if to be called on the Lin. RE sheets were in fact hoping much needed to make the Divisional ills the correct work.	

Army Form C. 2118.

WAR DIARY
or
INTELLIGENCE SUMMARY.
(Erase heading not required.)

Instructions regarding War Diaries and Intelligence Summaries are contained in F. S. Regs., Part II. and the Staff Manual respectively. Title pages will be prepared in manuscript.

Place	Date	Hour	Summary of Events and Information	Remarks and references to Appendices
Zegveldcappel	14/1/19		fort and flank of our forms of fire in the western by 215 and as Knott Zyphelia were proceeded on Demobilisation	
near Lillers	15/1/19		Lorfourts Station & Speakers tinned. Elements attended also orders received for the work to be Revision Camp on the 17th ms to posting of Men prevents the atmosphere	
	16/1/19		Lectures, Platoon and associated training thereafter. Exercises also completed for a proposed Divisional boxes tournament handed into 250 Brigade for training. It was hoped to hold a grand contest at Fletcher's Theatre. The outside judges judging the some of performers of hitters before the question of gallit believe was the Z.H. 15/83 though Captain this held to be another way in which the z.h.s. 15/83 meant was running from the all later hills the intervening week no moves failing	

WAR DIARY
or
INTELLIGENCE SUMMARY.
(Erase heading not required.)

Army Form C. 2118.

Place	Date	Hour	Summary of Events and Information	Remarks and references to Appendices
Le Renclos	1/1/19		Battalion moved to T.F. R@ Y16 Z7.017 Camp (see diary office C9.12.11 attached)	Appendix. I
Camp			Men were accommodated in bivouac huts, the camp, which in	
near			this dead weather does not include any lighting arrangements. The	
Allouagne			Officers were accommodated in the Chateau directly opposite the	
			camp and were well warmed. The Chateau contain seven	
			Officers and officers of C Company already in billets	
			were allowed to retain them. For the functions ours	
			the Battalion had been in Ironeer a Civilian Affairs Area	
			was started. Almost's conditions and the anti-kilt	
			still (consequence of the two and anti noon as shown in	
			the almost total lack of furniture fumigs now to mention	
			lighting & heating arrangements did not let the unit	
			unmodifications that welfare may adverse annuvalences. Three	
			reparables for the open compound is and their way hard	
			hard demand's were made on the Quartermasters Staff	
			for extra blankets as consequence twenty one	

Army Form C. 2118.

WAR DIARY
or
INTELLIGENCE SUMMARY.
(Erase heading not required.)

Instructions regarding War Diaries and Intelligence Summaries are contained in F. S. Regs., Part II. and the Staff Manual respectively. Title pages will be prepared in manuscript.

Place	Date	Hour	Summary of Events and Information	Remarks and references to Appendices
Le Reveillon	17/1/19		men employed in Demolition.	
Camp	18/1/19		Day spent in Hard work. The Office was in complete occupation of the 620th Field Company R.E. removed with the Battalion. It freed the camp. At 12-00 the Divisional Commander inspected the camps. Officers were in their temporary lines & were either on employ or in fatigue duties. The inspection was chiefly confined in order that the Battalion could avoid the Divisional side. The football match, no. QUCHE. 2nd Battalion, versus the 18th Battalion London Regt. Battalion was marked to the ground after an impunity match involving 20 minutes extra play to allow a decision. The 22nd were again successful by 2 goals to nil. 2 Lieut Clement L. and Lieut. were proceeded on Demobilisation.	

WAR DIARY or INTELLIGENCE SUMMARY.

Army Form C. 2118.

Place	Date	Hour	Summary of Events and Information	Remarks and references to Appendices
	19/1/13	11.30	Church of England parade service in Recreation hut at camp at 11.30. Revered STEELE conducted the service. Roman Catholic service parade at 11.30 at the Lucania Allsops. Roman Catholic service in Allsops Church at 10.00. Men enlisting for duration have twenty four hours leave under 2nd Lieut E.C. Savard.	
	20/1/13		Sick men paraded on Demobilisation. Remainder spent on usual employments, every available man being employed on Fatigue Duties. Baths at Allsops completed for Drawn parties attached to the Battalion. During the evening number 2nd Lieut S.E. Coward. In the afternoon there was a practice attendance of the Silver diary officers and sergeants. The former turned out in full strength but there were only a little bit over 40 altogether. Sixty nine enlisted for nightlong volunteers. Sixteen men proceeded on Demobilisation.	

WAR DIARY
or
INTELLIGENCE SUMMARY.
(Erase heading not required.)

Army Form C. 2118.

Place	Date	Hour	Summary of Events and Information	Remarks and references to Appendices
	21/1/19		Working Parties in camp. Completion for Division – Cross Country Run learned under 2nd Lieut E.O. Lawrance Lt H. was later trained under the Regimental Sergeant Major. Some third of Divisional Ship the Runners at BUCHER I/Sep Ground. The 22nd reserves the 167th Division Lewis Gun Battalion Result in Draw in spite of 14 minutes extra time freely played. The teams to afterwards met our team forward in and a memorable upper carried New Meagh fighters was proceeded in Demobilisation	
	22/1/19		Battalion less D Company proceeded to BUCHER – Elephant found for Brigade parade, every available man employed. D Company proceeded to CANTRAINE to Marselle old Horses lines belonging to M TERNOY leaving LE REVIERCON at 08.00 hours and returning during the afternoon	

Army Form C. 2118.

WAR DIARY
or
INTELLIGENCE SUMMARY.
(Erase heading not required.)

Instructions regarding War Diaries and Intelligence Summaries are contained in F. S. Regs., Part II. and the Staff Manual respectively. Title pages will be prepared in manuscript.

Place	Date	Hour	Summary of Events and Information	Remarks and references to Appendices
	23/1/18		Battalion working party under order R.E. arrangements.	
15 REVEILLON			"A" Company proceeded to CHATTRIX on working party. "B" Company having marched to LIGNY - at 10am yesterday, during the evening "B" Company proceeded to CHATTRING - "B" Company working	
Camp	24/1/		"B" working party - B working party - Work on coal factory finished, London Gazette dated 21st January 1918 published the following Lower decad -	
			682018 C.S.M.S. Box 5th 19 Rey - 68 0268 Sergt Weldin C2 B - 68 3689 L/C Donington C2 2nd 69 305- Walten C4 S4.	
			Immediate cross warrded men Walters and L/Cpl Mc Lyon found in ichny a the RUCHET flying ground	
			L/Cpl J Mec Baller Lipton M2	

WAR DIARY
or
INTELLIGENCE SUMMARY.

(Erase heading not required.)

Army Form C. 2118.

Place	Date	Hour	Summary of Events and Information	Remarks and references to Appendices
Dunkirk	29/4/19		Arrived in Dunkirk.	
	29/4/19		Men working parties carried on as usual. The camp Educational Classes attend the Recreation Room.	
	30/4/19		F.A. Shoe was held in the Recreation Room. Twenty Three men paraded for Dumbarton Battalion paraded for Church of England service in the Recreation Room at 11:30. Revered F.R. Chapel conducted the service. Roman Catholic at 09:00 and 10:00 at Church. Church conformists at 09:45 in Church hut. 16th London Field Ambulance at Church Lieut Col King M.C. and twenty two men proceeded on Dumbarton.	

WAR DIARY
or
INTELLIGENCE SUMMARY.

Army Form C. 2118.

Place	Date	Hour	Summary of Events and Information	Remarks and references to Appendices
	27/1/19		Work and families carried on in the camp. Church Parade Central N.E. on usual party. Chaps of the 150th Bearrers Corps took divine service. During the evening in the Recreation room an audit hired to be entirely of officers sergeants secured received the tickets and 1st, 2nd, 3rd, awarded the money. Amount of energy was little in the afternoon by the chiefs weather knew to Bilojan 20.9/42/9/3 Pte Wilson Bilojan. The General Officer Commanding the 142nd Infantry Brigade inspected the camp in the morning. Twenty men proceeded to Dunkirk this.	

Army Form C. 2118.

WAR DIARY
or
INTELLIGENCE SUMMARY.
(Erase heading not required.)

Instructions regarding War Diaries and Intelligence Summaries are contained in F. S. Regs., Part II. and the Staff Manual respectively. Title pages will be prepared in manuscript.

Place	Date	Hour	Summary of Events and Information	Remarks and references to Appendices
AT RENFLION	28/1/19		Working parties on the Route D Company proceeded to CANTRAINNE	
Camp			on working party. Remainder of the Battalion under Company	
			arrangements. All leave guns, spare parts and magazines	
			handed in from the Companies to the Armourers Shop.	
			Eighteen men proceeded on Demobilisation.	
	29/1/19		Working parties on the camp. A temporary boarded	
			floor was put into the hut where by Captain	
			to CANTRAINNE. A lecture on Labour problems	
			after the war which was to be given by Captain	
			a Patron at 17.00 in the Recreation Room was	
			postponed.	
	30/1/19		The Battalion worked under Company arrangements.	
			Games & Sports. Elementary education lessons	
			& shorthand classes were held during the morning	
			The results of the Board of Enquiry held recently	
			on the loss of stores at Clenades of the	
			Divisional Gardens, & the accounts of proficiency	

WAR DIARY or INTELLIGENCE SUMMARY

Army Form C. 2118.

Place	Date	Hour	Summary of Events and Information	Remarks and references to Appendices
LE RÉVEILLON	30/1/19		was insufficient on application of Lee Saulter who complete Evacuation of Laferté à Patereon. Six Captain à Patereon or "Sabon fondling" were join at 17.20	
Camp near LIZIERS	31/1/19		Inspection of Infantry Company Commander's arrangement. Inspected the indents of Messrs of the Company. Labour & Motor mechanics held on the wagons. A Battalion run of about 8 miles took place at 15.20. The run was voluntary. All there was a great afternoon. Twelve men proceeded on Demobilisation. During the month of January 4 Officers & 290 other ranks left the Battn. To be demobilised & 68 other ranks were discharged in England. The total numbering away from the company of December were 6 Officers and 367 other ranks.	

O.C. 1/22nd London Regiment (The Queens)

F. Thompson
Lieut Colonel
O.C. 1/22nd London Regiment (The Queens)

WAR DIARY or INTELLIGENCE SUMMARY

Army Form C. 2118.

(Erase heading not required.)

Instructions regarding War Diaries and Intelligence Summaries are contained in F. S. Regs., Part II. and the Staff Manual respectively. Title pages will be prepared in manuscript.

Place	Date	Hour	Summary of Events and Information	Remarks and references to Appendices
Le Havre	1/2/19		Sports class in 5th Bn. Received B.M. arrangements in morning.	
Camp			Provisional notes tending arrangements up to 11.00.	
			Lecture or conference to the Colonel by Capt Witherin in Mess Lecture at 11.00	
			Arrangement made to send 15 N.C.O's as competitors whole day Relay races but owing to inclement of weather the Recreation training had to be postponed.	
	2/2/19		The seated for the optionally all to be to Div Rest Camp Cadeau at 10.15	
			Church of England Lance Leman in Mess Canteen at 10.15	
			Roman Catholic Parade to Lavies Church Arragges Mass 07.00 10.00 Benediction 19.30	
			John communion in 3rd Bn Recreation this afternoon	
			The Barracks tomorrow in Supplies the Division Rugby game had to be postponed	
	3/2/19		25 ot to Div Rest Camp of Dunbreytin	
			Elementary Education class started today	
			Voluntary Shorthand class in morning	
			Recreational games arranged to take place on the field but had to be abandoned owing to the rapid multiplying tendency of the weather.	
			No Demobilization this day.	

Army Form C. 2118.

WAR DIARY
or
INTELLIGENCE SUMMARY.
(Erase heading not required.)

Instructions regarding War Diaries and Intelligence Summaries are contained in F. S. Regs., Part II. and the Staff Manual respectively. Title pages will be prepared in manuscript.

Place	Date	Hour	Summary of Events and Information	Remarks and references to Appendices
1. Reveillon	4/2/19		Elementary Education. Motor Mechanic Class held in hants.	
Allonne			Brigade Interkepert class at Allonne (2nd Bn Recreation Hut) at 10.00	
			Remainder of Companies under Coy arrangements	
			Weather still very cold	
			No developments this day	
	5/2/19		Elementary Education Platoon classes in morning	
			Remainder under Company arrangements. Particular attention being paid to Horsemanship	
			10 O.R. to Div Recpln Camp for Shakingbown	
			Elementary Education during morning	
			Voluntary sports Class in 2nd Bn Recreation Hut Allonne at 10.00	
	6/2/19		Given then accounts adnate	
			Result of Company Cortig competition in this Brigade:–	
			1st. Bn. 2nd B Coy. 2nd A Coy. 4th D Coy. 5th The Coy.	
			Prizes in cash were given to the Cos & the Comps of winning Cos. receive instructions to fight to Div HQ to collect his prize. The chair managed the selt conceptually Camps had to spin hi aid in the Camp	
			a filling Impostary Bond to fine Probed out in the Camp at 10.50 return tonight burn down the Electric light 2hd, and ashley	

Army Form C. 2118.

WAR DIARY
or
INTELLIGENCE SUMMARY.
(Erase heading not required.)

Instructions regarding War Diaries and Intelligence Summaries are contained in F. S. Regs., Part II. and the Staff Manual respectively. Title pages will be prepared in manuscript.

Place	Date	Hour	Summary of Events and Information	Remarks and references to Appendices
Cravillers			30 OR to Div Recpts Camp of Demobilgaton	
Allonye	7/2/19		Elementary Education in morning	
			Bookkeeping Class 24th Bn Decadors Ord orange at 10.00	
			Remainder under Coy and arrangements	
	8/2/19		21 O.R. to Div Recpts Camp for Demobilgaton	
			Elementary Education at 09.00 – 10.00	
			Baths into parties during morning	
			8 OR to Div Recpts Camp for Demobilgaton	
			10 hand "Officers and men who wish to attend a performance of 46th Divnl	
			Minstrels "Alpha Bates" 1440 books at Cinema Theatre in evening. Lgth	
			Canteen funds defrayed the expenses	
	9/2/19		Church of England Service in Bxx bearing at 11.30	
			Voluntary amount in camp at 17.30	
			Roman Catholics in Parish Church Allonye	
			No Parties with at 6th Coy RE Duntin Allonye at 10.40.	
			7 O.R. to Div Recpts Camp of Demobilgaton	

Army Form C. 2118.

WAR DIARY
or
INTELLIGENCE SUMMARY.
(Erase heading not required.)

Instructions regarding War Diaries and Intelligence Summaries are contained in F. S. Regs., Part II. and the Staff Manual respectively. Title pages will be prepared in manuscript.

Place	Date	Hour	Summary of Events and Information	Remarks and references to Appendices
Edmonton	10/2/19		Elementary Education during morning. Evening under lecp arrangements. Orders were put during the afternoon. Information received that Lt. (A/Cap) Wild broke me wanted Belgian Decoration "Chevalier de l'Ordre de Leopold" & "Croix de guerre". No demobilization this day.	
	11/2/19		Elementary education class in morning. Remainder under lecp arrangements. Boys stuck me retired forth. At 12.00 this day the Coys "X and Y" were amalgamated and formed "Z" Coy. This coy was commanded by Capt. A.L. Battley.	
	12/2/19		Elementary Education during the morning. Lect under lecp arrangements. I att. demobilized (to Dis Reception Camp) Lecp under lecp arrangements. The men leave the Camp and report to a police picquet H.N. to Dis Recept Camp for Demobilization	

WAR DIARY
or
INTELLIGENCE SUMMARY.
(Erase heading not required.)

Army Form C. 2118.

Place	Date	Hour	Summary of Events and Information	Remarks and references to Appendices
Quevillon	14/2/19		Intra bay movements and fatigue work	
Allonagne	15/2/19		4 oR to Div Reception Camp for Demobilisation	
			Elementary education class in session	
			Remainder of men employed on fatigue work in the Camp	
			Mr Dewr Esq. Sh. together with one Corps proceeds to La Recouits to complete absentee trial there	
	16/2/19		2 OR 15th Div Recept Camp for Demobilisation	
			Joint Service of Evelyne Parade service with 25th Battn in Gym Centre at 11.30	
	17/2/19		5 OR to Div Recept Camp for Demobilisation	
			Owing to the number of men employed away from the Camp on Investigation duties, Guards, Div HQ Guards and sorting parties etc it was found to be impossible for the moment with the smaller number of men available to do any other work other than fatigue duties in the Camp	
	18/2/19		Elementary Education class in the morning	
			Sundry fatigues in the Camp	

WAR DIARY or INTELLIGENCE SUMMARY

Army Form C. 2118.

(Erase heading not required.)

Instructions regarding War Diaries and Intelligence Summaries are contained in F. S. Regs., Part II. and the Staff Manual respectively. Title pages will be prepared in manuscript.

Place	Date	Hour	Summary of Events and Information	Remarks and references to Appendices
Education	19/2/19		Education takes during the morning. Baths in the Camp & lectures to "Z" Coy during the day. From 1030 the Div H.Q. and Div Headquarters were found by us daily. 3/2d Hampshire (& Div Receipts Camp) all available men employed on fatigue work in the camp	
	20/2/19		Baths resorted to Hampshire's [?] during the afternoon. At the & Div Reagts Camp & Hempstingten. Elementary Education class in camp at 10:30. Divl Compass on which the camp & conducted were organised. Recreation clubs to be arranged to the afternoon. As carriers for see rackets & programme of outdoor recreation was necessarily meagre only those man employed on essential administrative duties being spared recreation in the afternoon.	
	21/2/19			
	22/2/19		3/2d Hampshire (& Div Receipts Camp). Elementary Education in Regt continued at 10:30. There was a short voluntary Battn run in the afternoon, the attendance was somewhat meagre. 2nth to Div Receipts Camp & Hempstingten.	

WAR DIARY
or
INTELLIGENCE SUMMARY.

(Erase heading not required.)

Army Form C. 2118.

Place	Date	Hour	Summary of Events and Information	Remarks and references to Appendices
Menin	22/2/19		Church of England Parade Service in Camp at 11.00	
Antwerp	23/2/19		No intelligence. The rest of the day being spent in Barracks.	
			Elementary Education Class during the day	
			Intention Payment touring at 1000 under Lt. Col Whitcher	
			1st Gloster and 2/20 Bn returned from Le Havre and being relieved by 1/6	
			The Queens Regt. This means of one ration of 100. a certain amount of	
			Hanging to be done daily	
			There was a Battn. picture match in the afternoon. Cake v the Rest	
			at which the Rest were surprise.	
			No intelligence	
			Inspection Skeleton leaf drill v attack inclus formed at 10.00	
			Elementary Education Class	
			Battn. rifle class in afternoon a slightly stronger form of movement	
			the basis supplying a master follows for frequent field	
			No intelligence	
	24/2/19	07.30	Inspection at 07.30	

Re: Reveillon
Allouagne

Musketry practice on Allouagne range in conjunction with 12 Pl. 2 Bn. Ly. Rgt. Elementary Education 09/30

Inspected match during the afternoon, there was some little doubt as to whether this match would materialise owing to the difficulty experienced in finding in which capital of taking the fracture. Eventually a 13 man platoon performed this purpose.

22/2/19. Inspection. Physical training. Bayonette fighting 10.00
Bns allotted to 'Z' Company the morning
Three Baths from in afternoon.
4 or to Dir Drafts Camp to Doullens.

23/2/19. Elementary Education 09.30
Inspection. Skeleton bat line 10.00
Baths numerous on this service & General section.
Other votes in afternoon. Queen's Bolton V. The Rest
was by the 2nd latter. Other water to the purpose of selecting a
Brn Cadre team who played on Aracot ground, following players from the
units.
A. Getesto. Pte Limfield
H. Floyd. Pte Limfield
Pte Murphy Pte Yates.
7 or 6 Dir Drafts Camp to Doullnighton.

Smith
Capt Armin.
Acy. Cat. (A.P.S.)

Dr. Cellidge

| Sheridan Amaya | 17/9 | Continued.
The Rev. Sillis gave two last performances of this Java pantomime at above theatre. Nothing day now than half the number intending see the original members were being demobilized. At the conclusion of the performance the Prince handed thanks in the name of the Dutch to all thanks they had done in the scheme and emphasised how of thanks wartime to amuse and entertain no and noted them all the best of fortune on their return to civilian life.

During the month the 159 th Demobilized from the Rates Streets
to 13. M. Demobilized whilst on leave & from establish ordnce |

Herders Cook

Isaac Ben Casarly Major Comdg.

Army Form C. 2118.

WAR DIARY
or
INTELLIGENCE SUMMARY.
(Erase heading not required.)

Instructions regarding War Diaries and Intelligence Summaries are contained in F. S. Regs., Part II. and the Staff Manual respectively. Title pages will be prepared in manuscript.

Place	Date	Hour	Summary of Events and Information	Remarks and references to Appendices
LE REVIEZION	1/3/19	—	Inspection and Physical Training during the morning followed by general fatigue work in the camp. All officers were Brevet and S/Sergt went as a Guard Guard because of the sniper variety contest. Major H took M.C. Recreation on the afternoon into the form of a paper chase. This was rapidly becoming one of the arms strenuous form of amusement and the competition for the companies so keen that no whispers in turns very keen.	
	2/2/19		Church of England parade assemble in the Drug leader at 11.00 had summer this seemed 70 years so from everybody. G the 1st The Ditty Lack went within themselves at the time made the undergoing expression "Summer time" appears a little farcical but one could not help but admire the stick & thoughtfulness of those who however clean to do this thing when they already counted so the day	

Army Form C. 2118.

WAR DIARY
or
INTELLIGENCE SUMMARY.
(Erase heading not required.)

Instructions regarding War Diaries and Intelligence Summaries are contained in F. S. Regs., Part II. and the Staff Manual respectively. Title pages will be prepared in manuscript.

Place	Date	Hour	Summary of Events and Information	Remarks and references to Appendices
TF NEVILLON	2/2/19		in which we should be deprived of our Quarter Master chap. The Hanns Infantry Brigade beat our football team played the Divisional Headquarters team at BUSBUR? and lost.	
	3/2/19		Inspection of Public Company stall during the morning. Elementary Exercises also Football matches in the afternoon. Officers versus The Rest. The unfortunate Rest being commanded 2nd Lieut. um the Officers won.	
	4/2/19		Inspection of Platoons Elementary Squadron drill tactical exercises for officers under Major at 10am M.O. Then employed on fatigue work in the Camp Entries in the afternoon. It seems un—likely worth an apology by the? Staff was in rainy places, sitting behind and a supposed disguised so complete. French Governor came again! would to a laughing conclusion.	

Army Form C. 2118.

WAR DIARY
or
INTELLIGENCE SUMMARY.
(Erase heading not required.)

Instructions regarding War Diaries and Intelligence Summaries are contained in F. S. Regs., Part II. and the Staff Manual respectively. Title pages will be prepared in manuscript.

Place	Date	Hour	Summary of Events and Information	Remarks and references to Appendices
ZK REVIGION	5.3.19		Inspection & Musketry practice on ATOUAGNE Range. Elementary Education class. Football match at BURBURE for one Battalion versus R.A.S.C. Remainder performed usual movements with a Pack Mall. Orders received for all available available men as volunteers for any part of Doughton to the dets in various Spheres to go for Salvage Services at HAVRE.	
	6.3.19		Inspection. Battalion Company drill. Elementary Education class. Football match in the afternoon. The Officers who were selling on their return to Cowin in the affair of The Fox Inspection. Proposed choosing hierarchies of allowance including the 1st toddlers days. Paper chase during the afternoon rendered into pieces by an apparent lapse of memory on the part of the hares who quite failed to lay any paper. but at all eveners so after all those were perhaps somewhat in their madness.	
	7.3.19			

Army Form C. 2118.

WAR DIARY
or
INTELLIGENCE SUMMARY.
(Erase heading not required.)

Instructions regarding War Diaries and Intelligence Summaries are contained in F. S. Regs., Part II. and the Staff Manual respectively. Title pages will be prepared in manuscript.

Place	Date	Hour	Summary of Events and Information	Remarks and references to Appendices
Ft REVIGNON	8.3.19		Inspection & Physical training. Lectures economy Tactical scheme for officers. Rest all week during the afternoon. Motor buses out daily those wishes went to IZZERS for tea.	
	9.3.19		Church Parade parade service at 11.00 a.m. One leave out to Cabins for dispatch to England.	
	10.2/9		Inspection & Physical training. Lecture parties on clearing up the camp. Elementary Education class. Football watch won the afternoon the Coy of Occupation forming Roofront for the Riot. One side went to BETHUNE	

WAR DIARY

PLACE	DATE	SUMMARY OF EVENTS	
ZE REVIEZZOOI	11/3/19	Inspection and Physical Training. Tactical exercise for officers. Elementary Education classes. Rugger Union during the afternoon. In the evening the "Red Dominos" gave a performance in the Boys' Dining Hall. It could not un[der] any circumstances be called a high class entertainment. Possibly the kindest thing one can say about it is that our men received in warmer and confidence the performance were a little inclined to over estimate the quality of their efforts.	
	12/3/19	Inspection and Musketry practice on ALLOURGNE range. Elementary Education classes. Football match at BURBURE. The 42nd Battalion were defeated by Divisional Transport Command C.A.S.C. Revailler in a few Divisions have transport command and were husband.	
	13/3/19	Inspection and Infantry Drill. Brigade Tactical exercise with all Commanding officers, Adjutants and one husband. Commander for Battalion. Such being orders received by the 42nd Battalion from 10th Brigade following to contain the following morning the following were selected to proceed with it. Day at FERNES.	

WAR DIARY

SUMMARY OF EVENTS.

PLACE	DATE	
T.E. RENIEZZON	13/3/19	Lt. J.D. Hamilton M.C., 2nd Lt. R.W. Linnell, 2nd Lt. E.S. Lewis.
	14/3/19	Draft of 97 other ranks with Lt. J.D. Hamilton, 2nd Lt. R.W. Linnell and 2nd Lt. E.S. Lewis left camp at 09.45. Their departure left the Battalion very nearly at skele strength with the exception of officers of whom there were still a vast superfluity. The 4/4th Devonian Follies (a revised edition) gave a performance in the large Dining Hall. Audiences were necessarily somewhat smaller but what was lacking in numbers was more than made up in enthusiasm. Lifter our previous experience with "Lunatic" concert parties we were greatly surprised.
	15/3/19	Owing to the greatly reduced numbers any parade was quite impossible. Officers took part in a small tactical scheme. The afternoon was devoted to a Lecture by a

War Diary

SUMMARY OF EVENTS.

PLACE	DATE	
ZE REVIEZON	15/3/19	Stenuous order. In the evening an officers' armoury dinner was held at the Hôtel de la Paix XXXXXXS. All original 1/200 officers who originally reported with the division were present and the evening was entirely successful. The Public Cordial "between several distinguished officers and the alarming proficiencies of the C.O.'s being maintained with great sternuness.
	16.3.19	Church of England Parade service in Dry Barlen at 11.00 hrs. Roman Catholic Service at AZZOUAGNE 09.00 to 12.00 hrs. Special anniversary service (Church of England) at Division School Parades at 18.00 hrs. Preliminary order warning that the Colors of the Division would commence returning on the 23rd n.t.
	17.3.19	Inspection & Physical training. During the morning General fatigue work in camp - collection of rubbish

WAR DIARY

SUMMARY OF EVENTS.

PLACE	DATE	
TERUIKTON	17.3.19	Officers bathing to report on the Recreation Ground.
	18.3.19	Inspection & Physical training. Tactical exercise for all officers (written). Trial lads at that issued. The Orderly Room Staff breaker freely are Crown Information received of the undermentioned award.
		680705 Sergt J.F. SKIRTON M.M. Chaux de Violets Militaire 1st Class
	19.3.19	Inspection & interior economy. A Lorry was allotted to 'A' Coy to move all the stores & equipment to Thranghar where it was to be loaded on vehicles already parked there when the loading was complete all the vehicle of the 140nd Infantry Brigade were to be parked at FERNES. & there await entrainment. Fine this week.

WAR DIARY

SUMMARY OF EVENTS.

PLACE	DATE	
LE RIVIERSON	19.3.19	Proceeded to England for Demobilisation
	20.3.19	Inspection & Physical training. Heavy rain.
	21.3.19	Inspection & Physical training in the morning. The carting of vehicles at PERNES under arrangement was started. The last Battalion was concerned. G.O.C. Lobey was sent to 14th Battalion Head Quarters to remain there & be in charge of all vehicles and equipment belonging to this unit at PERNES. A paper stove is the [illegible] turn to individual trouble in [illegible] moves turn received that all movement of [illegible] to [illegible] was Wimberly cancelled.
	22.3.19	Inspection & Physical training. Bath allotted to all personal in camp. One hour & four Ridel[?]

WAR DIARY

SUMMARY OF EVENTS.

PLACE	DATE	
TE RIVIERON	22.3.19	Sent. K. KIZZERS for role.
	23.3.19	Church of England parade service in Dry Canteen at 10-30. Roman Catholic service in ATTOUAGNE at 09-30. Few Provisional date for the entrainment of the Battalion given as the 28th. Cinema prepared its usual the admitted with a certain amount of exception.
	24.3.19	Inspection & route march in the morning. Purple Lodes consisting of the Brigade Major & 10 Other ranks from the Battalion todays. The Lodes being received under the command of Lieut. Col. C.F.H. GREENWOOD D.S.O.
	25.3.19	T.D. Inspection. Physical training. Sports taken place in the afternoon. Supervision by the Qualmate Master at Infants of Railway Transport the Lodes wind

Place	Date	
LE RIVETON	25.3.19	Parade to the Brae by a series of paper chases was received with the contempt it deserved.
	26.3.19	Lieut. G.S. GREGORY D.C.M. M.M. proceeded on demobilization. Inspection and Physical Training during the morning. Information as to the move of the Brigade was rapidly becoming more and more vague and everyone was fast settling down to a further period of "wait-and-see." Lieut. F. WEAVER M.C. and three O.Rs. went to proceed on demobilization.
	27.3.19	Very heavy rain and snow storm. Indoor economy. A farewell dinner was given by the Divisional Commander to all commanding officers with the Division.
	28.3.19	Brigade parade at FROGINSHED at 12.15 when the Divisional Commander said farewell to all ranks. This day the 47th Division ceased to exist as such and the

WAR DIARY

SUMMARY OF EVENTS.

PLACE	DATE	
LE RIVIERON	28.3.19	4th Brigade Group of tanks came under the command of Brigadier General Kilner C.B. C.M.G. D.S.O. A bitterly cold day and a little fatigued FRIMINGHAM men and six mules from his camp Rue with wants proceeded on demolition Inspection and Physical training. Weather cold and
	29.3.19	very windy.
	30.3.19	Church of England Service in D.H. Canteen at 10-30. Roman Catholic service in Church at OZZOUARIC from 09.00 to 10-00 hrs.
	31.3.19	Inspection and Physical training. Further Leave life advance to 10.2nd Brigade Leave though played the 14th Brigade at PEREDY and got orders received for

WAR DIARY

PLACE	DATE	SUMMARY OF EVENTS.
LE TREPORT	31.3.19	The remaining available men for posting to the 1st Middlesex Regiment to be left in readiness to proceed on the 2nd June.
		Captain A.F. BUTWAY
		Lieut. M.S. DAVENPORT
		Lieut. A.P. HAYES
		proceeded to England on demobilisation.

C.H. Trumoor
Lieut Col
Commanding 1/22nd London Regiment
(The Queens)

Army Form C. 2118.

WAR DIARY
or
INTELLIGENCE SUMMARY.
(Erase heading not required.)

Instructions regarding War Diaries and Intelligence Summaries are contained in F. S. Regs., Part II. and the Staff Manual respectively. Title pages will be prepared in manuscript.

Place	Date	Hour	Summary of Events and Information	Remarks and references to Appendices
Tr NEWINGTON	1-4-19		Inspection and Sports Parade during morning.	
	2-4-19		Inspection and Physical training. Baths allotted to all ranks in evening.	
	3-4-19		Inspection and Physical training. Football match in the afternoon between 142nd Bn and 140th Infantry Brigade Group. Recreation in camp.	
	4-4-19		Inspection forenoon. Men employed in clearing up the remaining salvage around camp.	
	5-4-19		Inspection and Interior Economy.	
	6-4-19		Church of England Parade Service and Roman Catholic Service in Allonzy-au-Chauss at 09.30.	

Army Form C. 2118.

WAR DIARY
or
INTELLIGENCE SUMMARY.
(Erase heading not required.)

Instructions regarding War Diaries and Intelligence Summaries are contained in F. S. Regs., Part II. and the Staff Manual respectively. Title pages will be prepared in manuscript.

Place	Date	Hour	Summary of Events and Information	Remarks and references to Appendices
LE RUSSION	7-11-19		Interior Economy. Football match in the afternoon. The Battalion versus X1 Corps Cyclists. Draw in a tie.	
	8-11-19		Fatigue work in camp.	
	9-11-19		Fatigue work in camp.	
	10-11-19		Fatigue work in camp.	
	11-11-19		Interior Economy. Football match in the afternoon. Band plays versus X1 Corps Cyclists at Allouagne. Result a win for the Battalion.	
	12-11-19		Interior Economy. Orders received for all remaining men of 1st Middlesex Regt to proceed by train from PERNES	

(A7833) Wt W809/M1672 50,000 4/17 D. D. & L., London, E.C. **Sch. 52a** Forms/C/2118/4

WAR DIARY
or
INTELLIGENCE SUMMARY.
(Erase heading not required.)

Army Form C. 2118.

Place	Date	Hour	Summary of Events and Information	Remarks and references to Appendices
LE RAVEIRON	12-4-19		On the 14th inst.	
	14/4		Orders to Entrain Canada Reserve	
			for movement of Cadre received giving approximate date of	
			entrainment 19th inst. Two oven forwarded in Demobilization	
	13/4/19		Draft of 51 ORs proceeded to join 51 Middlesex having	
			arrived at 11.00 hrs. Appeared that this time the draw	
			would actually occur. All preliminary arrangements	
			made.	
	15/4/19		9 other ranks proceeded to England for Demobilization not being	
			the Battalion to practically Cadre strength. Appalling weather	
	16/4/19		Preparations made for the move of the Cadre to FROMINGHEM where	
			all the Surplus Cadres were to concentrate on 17 inst.	
			All surplus personnel despatched to Divisional Rest Camp.	
			Leaving the Battalion at exact Cadre strength.	

WAR DIARY
or
INTELLIGENCE SUMMARY.

Army Form C. 2118.

Instructions regarding War Diaries and Intelligence Summaries are contained in F. S. Regs., Part II. and the Staff Manual respectively. Title pages will be prepared in manuscript.

(Erase heading not required.)

Place	Date	Hour	Summary of Events and Information	Remarks and references to Appendices
LE PREVILLON	16.4.19 (contd)		All available men employed in clearing up the camp – lorries being allotted for all available stores. Slowness of move postponed until Army S.A. this was good. This was gradually becoming nearer to this somewhat complicated sort of date.	
	17.4.19		Divn moved to FLORINGHEM, leaving camp at 14.00 hrs. Lunch kept burning at this newformed unfolds of friendships made during the last three months. At FLORINGHEM the officers of the Brigade ran a combined mess as did the N.C.O.s & N.C.O.s - General feeling was also entertained for the men. it felt the conclusion did not appear hopeful, but one hoped for better things in the future.	
FLORINGHEM	18.4.19		System in vogue of each battalion finding all details for one day in rotation commencing with the 2nd Battn today. All available men employed on fatigue work in camp.	

WAR DIARY:

SUMMARY OF EVENTS.

PLACE	DATE	
FLORINGHEM	18.4.19	Voluntary Church of England service held in Church Army Hut PERNES.
	19.4.19	Baths allotted in PERNES to all Brigade personnel. Interior Economy.
	20.4.19	Voluntary Church of England service at Church Army Hut PERNES. Roman Catholic service in Church PERNES at 0900 hrs.
	21.4.19	Usual duties and fatigues for loading lorries allotted to also assist Delsaux Co. which have appeared to be a main quantity in the camp. Officially a holiday in the Rules Army in France and Flanders.

WAR DIARY.

SUMMARY OF EVENTS.

PLACE	DATE	
FREVINGHEM	22.4.19	Interior Economy. A gleam of light cast over a somewhat dark horizon by the army rumour that the entrainment of the Brigade Cadre Group would probably commence on the 28th inst.
	23.4.19	Interior Economy. Usual work on removal of salvage etc. A football match took place at FERFAY during the afternoon - 1142nd Cadre Group versus 1140: Cadre Group. Result a win 1 - 0.
	24.4.19	The departure of the train on 28th inst from PERNES was by this time a moral certainty. Work of clearing up salvage etc from camp progressed steadily.

WAR DIARY.

SUMMARY OF EVENTS

PLACE	DATE	
FOLKSHAM	25.4.19	Orders for the entrainment on 28th received. Events worth recording.
	26.4.19	All wagons of 1/22nd and 1/23rd Battalions were taken down to PURNES station and painted ready for loading. It began to look as if we nearly were going this time. Rough weather.
	27.4.19	No church service owing presumably to there being no Chaplain. Inspected batteloons during the day.
	28.4.19	Cadres of 1/22nd, 1/23rd Battalions 5 F. + 6 F. London Field Ambulances entrained at PURNES at 18.00 hrs.

WAR DIARY.

PLACE	DATE	SUMMARY OF EVENTS
	29-4-19	After a eventful slow journey the train eventually arrived at HAVRE at 19-30 hrs. Met by RTO and an officer from No 2 Reception Camp HARFLEUR. All vehicles were unloaded by civil personnel a guard left on them by his Battalion the remainder personnel marched to HARFLEUR (some 3 miles) arriving there at about midnight. Throughly tired and men incurred a lot sweat. All officers
HARFLEUR	30-4-19	All ranks bivouac and transferred to No 2 Dispatch Camp HARFLEUR to await a boat.
	1-5-19	All ranks confined to camp on account of Quay Day Labour demonstration in HAVRE

WAR DIARY.

PLACE	DATE	SUMMARY OF EVENTS.
HARFLEUR	2-5-19	Information received that an abortive outbreak in the evening. Lieut JP. POOLEY and working party of 10 O.R. proceeded 15 docks by lorry at 0700 hrs to assist in loading vehicles on SS ship. Sailed SS "PRINCE GEORGE" leaving HAVRE at 1900 hrs. Party very severely assaulted by a mob and stones thrown. Party very severely wounded and distinguished troops falling nearby working in "Land de mer".

Sgt Taber, a/s.
Capt & adjt for Lt Col.
Comdg 2/2nd Batt. The London Regt.
(The Queens)

"A" Form.
MESSAGES AND SIGNALS.

Army Form C. 2121.
(In pads of 100.)

Prefix	Code	in	Words.	Charge.	This message is on a/c of:	Recd. at .... m.
Office of Origin and Service Instructions.			Sent			Date ....
			At .... m.		.... Service.	From ....
			To			
			By		(Signature of "Franking Officer.")	By ....

TO — 142 Inf Bde Cadre G/s

Sender's Number.	Day of Month.	In reply to Number.	
*CY 158	6		AAA

Herewith War Diary completed as far as Date of Embarkation for May 2nd/19 England

From: 1/22" London Regt
Place: Cadre
Time:

W A Raby
Capt. od/c

* This line, except AAA, should be erased if not required.
Wt. W 3253/P511. 500,000 Pads. 1/18. B. & S. Ltd (E2389.)

21 Batt. London Regt.

H.Q. 140 Infantry Bde.

Herewith War Diary
for November.

M Catt?
Capt. & A/Adjt
for LT COL
     COMMANDING
     1/21st LONDON REGT

4/12/18

Appendix No 3.

Order No 205.

SECRET.

1/22nd Bn. London Regt Order No 205
Ref map Sheet 36 S.W.   3.10.18

1. 1/22nd Bn will move forward tonight and occupy
   line N.17.a.3.0 to N.23.c.5.0.
   Dispositions as follows. A Coy RIGHT
                            B "   RIGHT CENTRE
                            D "   LEFT CENTRE
                            C "   LEFT.

2. Battn will move off at 4.30 pm by Coys at
   200 yards distance in order H.Q. A, B, D & C Coy.

3. 2 Cooks per Coy together with sufficient dixies
   will proceed with Coys. Dixies will be carried
   by the men.

4. Rations will be sent up by pack mules
   tonight to N.23.a.5.3. Coys will each send
   2 men at 9.30 pm to ration dump, to unload
   pack animals if Bn has not arrived there
   or guide the rations forward if the Battn
   has moved. Rations will be collected under
   Coy arrangements.

5. Battn will be prepared at dawn tomorrow
   to pass through the right Battn of 175th
   Inf Bde. and continue the advance.

Distribution
   Usual.   1/22nd Bn London Regt

APPENDIX. Nº 4.

ORDER Nº 206.

SECRET.   Copy No
            1/22nd Bn. The London Regt Order No 20a.
Ref Map Sheet 36 SW.   3.10

1. 1/22nd Bn. London Regt will advance tomorrow passing
through the 1/18th Bn. London Regt which is at present
holding a line from O.14.cent. to O.20.cent.
On our left flank RADINGHAM is being held by the 141st
Inf Bde on our right flank the 74th Divsn are holding
the line O.20.d.0.0 to O.31.cent. Units on
both flanks are also advancing tomorrow morning.

2. Battn will leave present area at 4.30 am moving
by platoons at 50 yds distance in order B. A. D. & C. Coy.

3. 2 guns from 47th Bn M.G. Corps with personnel will be
attached to 'A' Coy and 2 to 'B' Coy. They will join
the Coys at 4.30 am on the main PROMELLE-LE-
MAISNIL ROAD in the Bn area

4. Route — Along MAIN LE-MAISNIL ROAD to road
junction O.B.d.1.9. thence South to O.19.d.0.0

5. Assembly position on road:-
    Dispositions :-
      RIGHT.   "B" Coy from O.19.d.0.0 to O.19.b.1.0.
      CENTRE   "A" "   "   O.19.b.1.0 to O.13.d.1.0
      LEFT.   "D" "   "   O.13.d.1.0 to X Rds. O.13.d.1.9.
      SUPPORT. "C" " 800 yds in rear of 'A' Coy
    Coys to be in position by 6.0 am

6. Battn will advance at 6.30 am direction due EAST.
Touch will be kept with the Centre Coy.

7. FIRST. OBJECTIVE The line O.15. central to O.21 central
which should be reached by 8.0 am.
FINAL OBJECTIVE Railway running N and South.

from O.16.b.7.7 to O.23.c.8.2 which should be reached by 10.0 am

8. "C" Coy will advance 800 yds in rear of Centre Coy and halt on a line approx 500 yds behind front line

9. After the Battn has reached the Railway, the 24th Bn London Regt. will pass through and continue the advance to the Canal. The 1/22nd Bn will then follow 1/24th Bn to pond from O.24.d to O.18.d. "C" Coy will again advance behind "A" Coy and halt 500 yds in rear.

10. Advance Bn HQ will open at approx O.13.d.3.7 where all reports and messages will be sent.

            Sgd. L.W. BROWN 7/9/1918
            1/22nd Bn London Regt.

Copy 1 File
    2 War Diary
    3 OC "A" Coy
    4 , "B" ,
    5 , "C" ,
    6 , "D" ,
    7 , "HQ" ,
    8 , C/oy 47 Bn M.G.C.
    9. Major O'Brien.

Appendix N° 5

Order N° 207.

SECRET.   Copy No IX
              1/22nd Bn. London Regt. ORDER No 207.
Ref map. SHEET 36 SW.   5.10.18

1. Battn will be relieved by the 23rd & 24th Bns London Regt tonight in accordance with schedule attached.
2. On relief Battn will move to LEMMASOUIL the billeted in shelters.
3. Guides from HQ will meet Coys at O.13.b.9.4. at 20.00 and guide them to billets etc.
4. All tools, SOS rockets & water cans will be carried out by Coys. All other stores will be handed over.
5. The 2 machine guns & personnel attached to each front line Coy will be handed over to their respective incoming Coy Comdrs.
6. Completion of relief will be reported to Advanced Bn HQ.
   Arrival in billets will be reported to rear Bn HQ.

                                        H R Cash
                                    1/22nd Bn London Regt.

Copy 1 file
     2 War Diary
     3 OC. A Coy
     4 ″ B ″
     5 ″ C ″
     6 ″ D ″
     7 ″ HQ ″
     8 RSM.
    10 OC. 24th Bn Lon Regt
    11 ″ 1/23rd ″

SCHEDULE.

1/22nd.	RELIEVING UNIT.	POSITION	REMARKS
A Coy.	D Coy 1/23rd	RIGHT FRONT.	Under arrangements to be made by OC. Coys concerned
B Coy.	—	RESERVE	Those remain in present position until 19.30 and then carry out work detailed separately.
C Coy	—	SUPPORT	Remain in present position until notification is received from O.C. A Coy 1/24th Lon Regt that his Coy is in position
D Coy	C Coy 1/24th	LEFT FRONT.	Under arrangements to be made by OC. Coys concerned.
Ad.B.HQ	Ad.B.H.Q 1/24	O. is d. 2.7.	On completion of relief move to Rear Bn. H.Q.

APPENDIX No 6.

ORDER No 208.

SECRET.   Copy No 2.

1/22nd Bn. London Regt. Order No 208.

Ref/Lat. 36 SW.   8.10.18.

1. 1/22nd Bn. will relieve 1/23 & 1/24 Bns in the front line tonight. Relief as per schedule.

2. Dress fighting order. Packs may be carried if OC Coys desire, if not they will be dumped centrally in their present camps and one man per Coy left as guard.

3. Coys will draw rations before they move off and carry them up. Waterbottles will be filled.

4. The 2 Cookers & water carts will when the Bn moves forward, move to the RED from at O.20.a.7.7.

5. All details of relief to be arranged by Coy Comdrs concerned.

6. Bn HQ will close at O.13.d.2.4. at 18.30 today and reopen on arrival at O.20.a.40.75.

7. Completion of relief will be notified to Bn HQ by code word LEAVE.

8. Tools if required may be drawn from Bn HQ.

                                  Sd. L. W. BROWN. 2/Lt 9/Adjt.
                                  1/22nd Bn London Regt.

Copy 1 File
     2 War Diary
     3 HQ 1/23rd Bn   8 OC D Coy
     4 ,, 1/24 Bn   9 ,, HQ ,,
     5 OC A Coy   10 RSM.
     6 ,, B ,,
     7 ,, C ,,

SCHEDULE

1/22nd Bn.	RELIEVE	POSITION	
1 Pltn. A Coy	1 Pl. C Coy 1/23	RIGHT. FRONT. (FL) O.22.a.8.7.	
1 Pltn. A /	1 / C Coy 1/24	do (FL) O.16.c.8.4.	
2 Plts A /	2 / A Coy 1/24	do (Supp) Chau Flandrin	to arrange by G.O. Conference
HQ A Coy	HQ A Coy /	Chau Flandrin	
1 plat. C Coy	1 plat D Coy 1/24	LEFT. FRONT. (FL) O.16 a cent.	
1 plat. C /	1 plat. D Coy 1/24	Do (FL) O.15b 7.7.	
2 plats C /	—	Do (Supp) opposite 72	
HQ C Coy.	—	Do O.16 a 75.75.	
B Coy	D Coy 1/23rd.	RIGHT. SUPPORT LEPLOVY	
D /	B Coy 1/24th.	LEFT SUPPORT O.14.a.18.6.	
Bn HQ	Bn HQ 1/23rd	O.20.a.40.75	

APPENDIX No 7.

ORDER No 209.

SECRET. Copy No 2

1/22nd Bn. London Regt. ORDER No 209.
Ref Sheet. 36 SW. /10.000.   10.10.18

1. INFORMATION. Enemy holds machine gun positions along the line of Embankment.

2. INTENTION. The 1/22nd Bn will raid area about O.17.c.0.0 to obtain identification.

3. RAIDING PARTY. 2/Lt G GREGORY DCM. M.M and one platoon B Coy.

4. OBJECTIVE. Area about O.17.c.0.0 with Northern Boundary on line passing E and W through O.17.c.0.4
Southern Boundary on line passing E and W through O.23.a.0.5.

5. POSITION OF ASSEMBLY. Pill Box at O.16.a.2.4.

6. JUMPING OFF POSITION: Bend of Railway at O.22.b.85.75

7. ACTION. Raiding party will leave position of assembly in time to be in position of assault at ZERO – 10. Party will leave position of assault at ZERO and will return at ZERO + 20 or before if prisoner has been obtained.

8. SIGNAL FOR RETURN. RED very light fired from Pill Box

9. PLACE OF RETURN. All raiders to return to CHAU DE FLANDRE and report to Lt O.H. DARLOT. M.C.

10. CO-OPERATION.
(a) Div. Artillery firing on Embankment North of O.17.c.05 and South of O.23.b.45 from ZERO to ZERO + 40.
(b) 6" T.M. Battery from ZERO to ZERO + 40 on target to

be fixed by OC. T.M.B.

(c) 3" T.M. Battery 2 guns from ZERO to ZERO +40 on houses along road O.16.d.8.8. 2 guns from ZERO +25 to ZERO +40 at the embankment within the picked area.

(d) Machine guns to fire on buildings E of Embankment from ZERO to ZERO +40.

11. EQUIPMENT. Rifles, Steel helmets, Box respirators, 10 rounds SAA and 1 bomb per man. No letters, shoulder titles etc to be taken.

12. MEDICAL. M.O. will open aid posts at CHAU DE FLANDRE with an advanced Station at Pill Box with 2 I.B's.

13. WATCHES. To be synchronized at Advanced Bn. H.Q. at 03.00am.

14. PRISONERS. To be sent under escort to CHAU DE FLANDRE

15. REPORTS. Reports from 19.00 10.10.18 until completion of operations to be sent to Advd Bn H.Q.

16. ZERO will be 04.40 11.10.18.

17. SIGNAL MANAGEMENT. Arrangements to be made with Sigs for message packets to be fired from Pill Box. OC. Sig. will arrange for enter phone line from Pill Box to Ad. Bn H.Q.

OC Sigs will arrange for RED coloured lights to be fired from vicinity of CHAU DE FLANDRE as a guide for Runners returning from ZERO +20 to ZERO +40.

APPENDIX. No. 9.

ORDER No 210.

SECRET   Copy No 2
           1/22nd Bn London Regt. Order No 210
Ref. Sheet 36 S.W.   11.10.18.

1. 1/22nd Bn will be relieved by 1/24th Bn in the line on night 11/12th
   October as per attached schedule.
2. On completion of relief Bn will withdraw to Billets at MAISNIL
3. All details of work in hand trench stores etc will be handed over
   with the exception of S.O.S signals, food containers & water cans
   which will be taken out by Coys. A receipt for all stores handed
   over to be sent to Bn H.Q by 12 noon 12.10.18.
   O.C Coys on relief will immediately send the S.O.S. rockets, which
   he took over from "D" Coy 24th Bn, to O.C. D Coy 24th Bn at O.pd 5.5
   60 Shovels & 40 picks only will be handed over by Ad Bn HQ and a
   receipt obtained. The remaining tools will be carried out.
4. O.C "C" Coy will send out a patrol which will patrol the Bn
   front & remains out until "C" Coy is relieved by 1/24th Bn.
5. Completion of relief will be notified to Battn HQ by code subject "SOCKS"
6. OC "D" Coy will work tonight as per separate instructions.
7. Bn. H.Q will move on completion of relief to O.13.a.75.10.

Copy 1 Filed   8 OC 1/24th Bn
     2 War Diary   9 M.O
     3 OC A Coy   10 T.O
     4 " B   11 QM   9/18 Adjt
     5 " C   12 R.S.M.   1/22nd Bn London Regt. (Queens)
     6 " D
     7 Ad Bn HQ

SCHEDULE.

1/22nd Bn	RELIEVED BY 1/24th Bn	POSITION	GUIDES	REMARKS
A Coy	A Coy	RIGHT FRONT	Will meet 24th Bn at 7.30pm. Place and other details to be arranged by OC Coys concerned.	
C "	B "	LEFT FRONT		
B "	C "	SUPPORT		
D "	D "	RESERVE	Will meet 22nd Bn at cross Roads MAISNIL	
Ad.B.H.Q	Ad.B.H.Q	CHAU. DE FLANDRE		
Bn.H.Q	Bn.H.Q	O.20.a.3.7.		

Appendix. N° 10.

Order N° 212.

SECRET: Copy No. []
              1st Bn London Regt Order No 2/2
Ref/Sheet 36SW & 36SE   15.10.18

1. The enemy having withdrawn from the front 23rd Bn
have advanced and are pushing fwd along line O.18 d O.6
to O.12 c [illegible]. When this land is made good 22nd Bn
[illegible] pass through. 23rd Bn on to the first Bde
Objective [illegible] from O.18 d 9.5 - P.13 c cent -
P.7 a 9.6 - P.7 d 0.5 with 22nd Bn on left
and 24th on right. On this objective being made
good 24th Bns come on to 2nd Bde Objective
which is the general line SEQUEDIN - CHAU
GRANDVILLE.

Bn Boundaries   Bde Southern O.20 d O.O - P.13 cent -
P.14 a 7.5 - P.11 a 6.3 - P.12 c 6.7 - P.18 a 6.0 -
P.18 d 3.5 thence East and to X [illegible] O.22 c 3.0
Bde Northern P.7 a O.O & thence NE along
[illegible] through P.1 d & b to J.32 a 7.7.
Inter Bn Boundary along line approx from
P.7 d O.O to P.2 d 2.4

2. Bn will attack in 2 Coy fronts each Coy
with 2 plats in front & in rear with C & D Coys
in front line (C on left) & A & B in support.
A Coy supporting C + B supporting D Coy.
On reaching first objective [illegible] advancing
plats to [illegible] A & B Coys [illegible] pass through
the attacking Coys to the 2nd Bde Objective & C & D
Coys remaining on the first objective.

3. Formation
(a) Attacking Coys 2 plats front line in line with

screen of scouts thrown well forward 2 posts in support. 200 yds distance between waves.
(b) Support Coy 300 yds behind attacking Coys sections in file.
(c) Machine Gun Sections attached to Bn will move immediately in rear of Support Coys to first objective from where the MG Sections will support the Advance to the 2nd Objective to the best ability.
4 Advanced report centre will be established at X Rds. P.17 b 2.9 until first objective is gained when Bn HQ will move to FIN DE LA GUERRE
5 Aid Post will be at ...
6 Prisoners will be conducted back to Bn HQ

Copy Nº

Distribution
1
2 Van Doos
3 R A Coy
4 " B "
5 " C "
6 " D "
7 Trench Mortar Bn
8 MG ... Section
9 ... Bde
10 Cap ...

Appendix No. 11.

Order No. 213.

SECRET   Copy No

1/2nd Bn London Regt Order No 213
Ref. Sheets 36 S.W. & 36 S.E.   15.10.18.

1. 23 Bde Advanced troops have reached
line O.12.c.9.2, O.18.a.9.3., O.18.c.55.60.
   The advance will be continued
by 22nd and 24th Battns tomorrow.

2. First and second objectives are as
explained in Order No 212 of to-day
3rd and final objective line of Canal
from P.11.a.5.3. J.36.d.9.1. and thence
to J.30.d.9.1.

3. Brigade boundaries as explained in
Order No 212 of to-day
  Inter Battn boundary O.18.b.1.5.
P.2.d.7.5. along road to X Rds P.4.b.3.8.
to P.6.b.2.8. 22nd Bn on left.

4. Formation. Battn will attack
with C & D Coys front line (C on left)
each on a 2 Platoon frontage protected
by strong screen of Scouts. B Coy
supporting D Coy and moving
300 yds behind the last wave

of D Coy and A Coy support C Coy and moving 200 yds behind and to the left of B Coy, Echeloned to protect the left flank of the advance

5. Barrage. At 05.45 Artillery will open fire on present S.O.S line p.7.a.65, p.7.d.15.40, p.7.d.35.00, p.13.b.35.35, p.13.b.30.00, p.13.d.50.50 and will stay in this line until 05.55 when it will creep forward for 1000 yds in a N.E. direction at 100 yds in every 4 minutes and then cease.

6. On reaching 2nd Objective and if the advance is still practicable A & B Coy will pass through C & D Coys to the 3rd and final objective moving approx due ~~East~~.

7. 22nd Bn will leave present line of Railway at 05.15. and will not pass East of line running N & S through p.7.a.0.0. until 05.45.

8. If enemy is encountered in force ground will be consolidated and no attempt will be made to attack him in force.

9. Plat HQ will be established in present combined Coy HQ and dig PsC in new posn.

10. Kitchen will be established by S.Q. at 05.00 at Coy H.Q.

11. 2 guns of M.G. Section will be attached to A Coy and R & B Coy to take knowledge.

Distribution as over.

[signature]

Appendix. 13.

Order No 217.

SECRET.   Copy No. II

[to] ...... O.C. Coys & Specialists ... Off.
O/Sect. 36 SW & M.W.   16.10.18.

1. 22nd Bn will be relieved by 2/6th and 2/7th Kings Liverpool
   Regt tomorrow 17th inst. Relief as per schedule.
   Immediately 2/6th & 2/7th Bns have taken over the line
   they will probably continue the Advance.

2. On relief or if as may be the case, the relieving troops
   pass through in attack formation the Battn will
   move to old Billetting areas in LEMAISNIL taking
   over previous dispositions. Dinners will be eaten
   at LEMAISNIL.

3. Coys will leave LEMAISNIL at approx 13:00 under
   orders to be issued later & proceed to FROMELLE by
   march route & entraining there for ????E area.

4. 2/Lt ??? will act as Entraining & detraining Officer.

5. Packs will be drawn at FROMELLE immediately
   on arrival there.

6. All petrol tins must be taken out of the line.
   Do not yet know whether transport will be available for
   Lewis guns.

7. Code subject relief complete EUROPE.

8. Movement to LEMAISNIL will be by parties of not
   more than half platoon strength at 200 yds distance

                                              [signature]

Duplicate
None

APPENDIX. Nº 14.

ORDER Nº 215

SECRET:-   Copy No 2

1/22ND BN LONDON REGT ORDER No 215

Mil. Sheets 36 and 36A   17.10.18.

1. B^{n} will entrain at FROMELLES STATION (N.23.6.5.4.) at 15.00 today leaving present area at 14.00. Detraining Station FOSSE. Movement by Coys at 200 yds distance in order. H.Q, A, B, C & D Coys.

2. Entraining Strength will reach this office by 13.00.

3. 2/Lt L.W. BROWN will act as Entraining Officer and will report to Bde. Entraining Officer at Station at 14.30.

4. Billeting Party of 2/Lt POOLEY and 1 N.C.O. per Coy & H.Q. will report to Batt^{n} H.Q. 13.00 ready to move.

5. Packs will be drawn at FROMELLES Station before entraining unless otherwise ordered.

Copy 1. File
     2. War Diary   P.K. Toby (?)
     3. O.C. A Coy   Capt & Adjt.
     4. " B "   1/22ND BN LONDON REGT
     5. " C "
     6. " D "
     7. " H.Q. "
     8. Capt Cook M.C.
     9. 2/Lt Brown
    10. 2/Lt Pooley
    11. M.O.
    12. R.S.M.

Appendix No. 15

Order No. 216

SECRET.   OPERATION ORDER NO. 216.   Copy No.

Refce. Map - HAZEBROUCK 5a 1/100,000.   17th October, 1918.

1. The Battalion will move by march route to BOURECQ to-morrow, 18th inst, passing Brigade Starting Point, Cross Roads West of FOSSE and 200 yards East of A in STA, at 0850 hours, in order H.Q., "D", "C", "B" & "A" Coys.
100 yards distance will be maintained between Coys.

2. Ten minutes halt will be made at each clock hour. There will be a midday halt from 1130 to 1300 hours, when dinners will be eaten.

3. Cookers and Lewis Gun limbers will march immediately in rear of Coys; remainder of Transport 100 yards in rear of last Company.

4. Two lorries are available for transport of packs, blankets, etc. Q.M. will detail guide to report at Brigade H.Q. at 0700 hours. Lorries may make two journeys if necessary.

5. Any men unable to march, to a maximum of 24 per Battalion, will be sent by the M.O. to Brigade H.Q. (BOUT-DEVILLE) by 0830 hours.

6. 2nd Lt. J.A. POOLEY will report at Battn H.Q. at 0830 ready to proceed billeting. A car will call for him.
A billeting party of 1 N.C.O. per Coy and M.Q. will proceed by cycle, leaving FOSSE at 0800 hours and reporting to the Staff Captain at the Church, HAM EN ARTOIS at 1200 hours.

7. Packs, valises, mess kit, etc. as ordered in my C.G.331 (Warning Order).

8. Route:- FOSSE - Cross Roads ½ mile S.E. of M in LESTREM - Road Junction South of L in LESTREM - CALONNE - ROBECQ - BUSNES.

                                            Capt. & Adjt.,
                                1/22nd Bn The London Regt. (The Queens).

Copy No. 1 - File.
        2 - War Diary.
        3 - Second in Command.
        4 - Adjutant.
        5 - Asst. Adjutant.
        6 - O.C., "A" Coy.
        7 - O.C., "B" :
        8 - O.C., "C" :
        9 - O.C., "D" :
       10 - Q.M.
       11 - T.O.
       12 - M.O.
       13 - S.O.
       14 - R.S.M.

SECRET.

Reference map Sheet 36.

1. 1/22nd Bn. The London Regiment will march through LILLE tomorrow as part of the 142nd. Infantry Brigade Group.

2. The following Transport will proceed in rear of the Battalion :-
   2 Cookers ("B" and "D" Company's)
   4 Lewis Gun limbered wagons.
   1 Water Cart.

3. Order of march of the Brigade Group :-
   Brigade Headquarters
   520th. Company Royal Engineers
   22nd. Bn. The London Regiment
   23rd. Bn. The London Regiment
   24th. Bn. The London Regiment
   142nd. Trench Mortar Battery.
   6th. London Field Ambulance.

   Order of march of the Battalion :-
   Drums
   "B" Company
   "C" Company
   "D" Company
   Transport
   Details will parade with their Companies.

4. Battalion will form up in column of route on main LOOS - LILLE ROAD facing East in above order with head of column at CONVENT (where "B" and "D" Companies are billetted) at 08.00 hours ready to move. Companies will be sized as for ceremonial.
   The following distances will be maintained between Units :-
   Between Battalions - 20 yards
   Between Companies - 10 yards

5. "A" Company will move off independently and will report at the PORTE DE CANTELEU at 09.30 hours

6. DRESS.
   All Officers will wear Sam Browne belt, revolver, box respirator (slung) and steel helmet. Dismounted Officers will not wear field boots.
   Other ranks. Fighting Order as previously laid down with box respirator slung. Bayonets will not be fixed.
   Battalion will march at attention from PORTE DE CANTELEU until after passing the GRANDE PLACE. No compliments will be paid to the Army Commander in the GRANDE PLACE.
   Haversack ration will be carried.

7. Surplus Transport and Personnel will proceed by march route under orders of Major Preston A.S.C. to new billetting area - LEZENNES and Q.12.
   Order of march :-
   520th Field Company Royal Engineers
   22nd Bn The London Regiment.
   142nd Infantry Brigade Headquarters.
   142nd Trench Mortar Battery.
   23rd. Bn. The London Regiment.
   6th. London Field Ambulance.
   24th. Bn. The London Regiment.
   No. 4 Company 47th. Divnl. Train A.S.C.
   250 yards will be maintained between Units.
   Starting Point :- Road Junction P.24.a.3.3.
   Head of column will pass Starting Point at 11.00 hours.
   Route :- ENNEQUIN - ROUCHIN - LEZENNES.

8. There will be a halt of 10 minutes at the Western end of the GRANDE PLACE while the Army Commander presents his standard to the Mayor of LILLE. During this halt troops will stand easy but will not fall out.

9. Orders regarding Officers Valises, packs etc. will be issued later.

                                                Captain & Adjutant.
                                  1/22nd Bn. The London Regiment.
                                      (The Queens.

Copy No 1. Filed
2. War Diary
3. 2nd in Comd.
4. Adjutant.
5. Ast Adjt.
6. O.C. "H.Q." Coy
7. O.C. "A" Coy.
8. O.C. "B" Coy.
9. O.C. "C" Coy.
10. O.C. "D" Coy.
11. T.O.
12. Q.M.
13. M.O.
14. R.S.M.

APPENDIX No 16

ORDER No 218.

SECRET.   Copy No

1/23nd. Bn. THE LONDON REGIMENT ORDER NO. 218.

Reference Maps Sheet 36 and 36A.   25 10 18.

1. 1/23nd Bn The London Regt. Less Transport will move by train tomorrow from LILLERS at 08.00 hours detraining at DON from where it will march to Billets in LOOS.

2. Battn. will pass point U.8.a.8.7 on LILLERS - BOURECQ road at 07.15 hours in order "H.Q." "A" "B" "C" and "D" Coys. 100 yards distance will be maintained between Coys.
   Dress. Full Marching Order.

3. Lieut O.H.DARLOT M.C. will act as entraining and detraining Officer and will report to Major A.TOTTON M.C. (the Brigade Entraining Officer) at LILLERS STATION at 07.30 hours.
   Entraining states will reach this Office by 18.00 hours today.

4. Two lorries for conveyance of blankets, surplus kit etc will be at Brigade H.Q. at 07.00 hours tomorrow.
   All blankets tightly rolled in bundles of 10, surplus mess kit, dixies etc. will be dumped at Q.M. Stores by 07.00 hours tomorrow.

5. Haversack ration and full water bottles will be carried.

6. O.C. Coys are responsible that all Billets are left in a clean and sanitary condition.

                                                    Capt & Adjt.
                                                1/23nd Bn The London Regt.
                                                    (The Queens).

Distribution :-
    Copy No 1. File
         2. War Diary
         3. 2nd in Comd.
         4. Adjt.
         5. M.O.
         6. T.O.
         7. Q.M.
         8. O.C. "H"Q." Coy.
         9. O.C. "A" Coy
        10. O.C. "B" Coy.
        11. O.C. "C" Coy.
        12. O.C. "D" Coy.
        13. R.S.M.

Appendix N° 17.
Order N° 220.

1/22nd Bn The London Regt. (The Queens).

Reference Operation Order No. 280.

(1) The Battalion will be on parade ready to move at 08.55 hours sharp and not 09.00 as previously stated.

(2) The Quartermaster will be in charge of the Transport which accompanies the Battalion.

(3) Guides for billets in the new area will be at road junction Q.5.c.8.0 at 11.30 hours. Battalion billeting area is on South side of road from Q.11.c.2.5 to Q.12.b.2.2.

(4) All packs, blankets and officers valises will be dumped at Q.M. Stores by 08.15 hours. Messtins will be packed _inside_ the packs. Service caps will be dumped by Coys at Q.M. Stores packed in bread sacks.

(5) All details not proceeding with the Battalion will report to the Transport Officer at the Transport Lines at 09.45 hours in Full Marching Order, carrying their rations for to-morrow.

(6) Officers will wear gloves. Sticks will not be carried.

(7) Stretcher Bearers will march in the rear of "D" Coy under the Medical Officer.

27/10/18.
O.O. 384.

Capt. & Adjt.,
1/22nd Bn The London Regt. (The Queens).

Distribution:- As for O.O. 280.

www.ingramcontent.com/pod-product-compliance
Lightning Source LLC
Chambersburg PA
CBHW081535160426
43191CB00011B/1766